THE DEMOCRACY DELUSION

How to Restore True Democracy and Stop Being Duped!

THE DEMOCRACY DELUSION

How to Restore True Democracy and Stop Being Duped!

BAY JORDAN

R3THINK PRESS

First Published in Great Britain 2013 by Bookshaker

Second Edition Published in Great Britain 2015 by Rethink Press

© Bay Jordan

All rights reserved. No part of this publication may be reproduced, stored in or introduced into a retrieval system, or transmitted, in any form, or by any means (electronic, mechanical, photocopying, recording or otherwise) without the prior written permission of the publisher.

This book is sold subject to the condition that it shall not, by way of trade or otherwise, be lent, resold, hired out, or otherwise circulated without the publisher's prior consent in any form of binding or cover other than that in which it is published and without a similar condition including this condition being imposed on the subsequent purchaser.

Cover image © www.istockphoto.com/imagestock

*To all those who have believed in me,
helped me and stood by me.*

PRAISE

"Although the points made in this book are expressed with passion and conviction, they are not personal rants but clear illustrations of our deluded leadership, under-pinned by data, evidence and powerful examples from all walks of life. From the inherent dysfunctionality of the Financial Services industry – especially Banking – to the perversities pursued in the name of democracy and the backward nature of Western education at a time when India and China will soon overtake the Western economies, this book urges us to challenge the assumption that what has made us successful in the past will continue to make us successful in the future!"

Peter Boggis, Founding Partner, Formicio Limited, helping organisations change their default future to one which is more acceptable and sustainable

"This is a radical thesis that looks at the paradox of conventional wisdom and lack of innovative solutions to the problems of the modern world. Its author has a solid background in understanding human capital and all that it could achieve, so to hear his views on where we are going wrong is insightful.

It resonates with the new movement for improved democratic models and Jordan poses the question "just how democratic are we?" He sets this against the economic and social impacts of man's behaviour over the last couple of centuries. Overall a damning indictment of modern economics and political process. His proposed solutions are enshrined in some simple principles and he shows how these might change the way we account for wealth, ownership and taxation. A thoughtful read and plenty to stimulate new thinking. You don't have to agree completely with what the author has to say but it is a useful base from which to challenge the financial ecosystem and make the world a better place."

Rob Wherrett, TD FRSA FInstLM, Social Entrepreneur and Management Expert who has been engaged with social improvement and radical change across the UK. He is Director of Consultancy for Zymolysis (part of the Lamberhurst Network) and author of 'The Compleat Biz'

"'The Democracy Delusion' doesn't pull its punches! What is refreshing about this book is that it combines a detailed analysis of the issues and causes with a carefully-considered, practical prescription to address them. The solution is deceptively simple, and undoubtedly powerful."

Dr Emma Langman, MEng (hons), PhD.
Change Magician and MD of Progression Partnership Ltd.

"Fingers crossed – that's all I can say. Well written and a good synopsis of the events of the last decade, offering a thoughtful approach."

DB Heslip, Burlington, Ontario, A Chartered Accountant who markets common sense

"'The Democracy Delusion' is an extraordinary and valuable book. It takes a 'no punches pulled' approach to reviewing the current state of democracy in the UK and other 'developed' nations. Not new so far. But the author also builds links between democracy and organisational management, and shows how taxation systems and conventional management thinking dilute real democracy for millions of people. The key, however, is that Bay Jordan goes far beyond the critical review and provides practical, working solutions to the key problems of organisational management, taxation and benefits. His ideas are innovative, radical and challenging - but bear with him and do not react without taking out time to think about them first. They actually make sense, and illuminate a sensible way forward. All that is needed to make them work is sensible and brave CEOs and politicians. Oh well, now there's a problem!"

Denis Bourne, Director, Magus Toolbox Limited

"A tremendous research effort. Any one reading this work would certainly have their archetypes challenged and it gives the reader much fuel for dialogue. I am delighted to find someone championing a dynamic and prosperous democracy going forward."

Mitch Krayton, Speaker, Coach, Author, Consultant;
President and Founder, Krayton Seminars and Partner, Krayton Travel

"Today the world's great democracies face political, economic, and environmental crises which threaten the future of democracy itself and the future of each of us. The threats of revolution, economic collapse, and environmental disaster stand at the door. And the door is wide open.

Yet the politicians and leaders, their plans and initiatives, seem too small for the job. Looming crises dwarf polite proposals. Nobody seems to see big-picture problems clearly and address them on a meaningful scale.

Few people have the breadth of vision and experience to see across multiple continents to the true big picture. Bay Jordan--to our great benefit – does just this. He brings uncommon clarity of vision to the problems that confront and threaten both us and our democracies. He challenges conventional misconceptions and argues forcefully for his proposed solutions – solutions which will engage the intellect of corporate and political leaders and prompt inspired and meaningful action. Our democratic way of life and economic security are at stake now. Read 'The Democracy Delusion' today."

Eric Troseth, JD; MBA

CONTENTS

Foreword by Lawrence Bloom
Preface

Introduction	1
PART ONE: MISPLACED CONVENTIONS	7
1. Upside-down Democracy	9
2. The Erosion of Equality	23
3. Awful Accounting	43
4. Permitted Plunder & Legalised Larceny	47
5. Policy Perversion	55
6. Errant Education	65
7. Diseconomies of Scale	75
8. Sabotaging the State	85
9. The Emperor's New Clothes	95
PART TWO: OVERARCHING PRINCIPLES	103
10. Building on Principles	105
PART THREE: REFORMING SOLUTIONS	113
11. A New Accounting Regimen	115
12. A New Tax Regimen	131
13. A New Democracy	153
14. A New Sustainability	163
Epilogue	169
Afterword	171
Appendix: People as Assets – An Objection Overcome	195
About The Author	198

FOREWORD

In life timing is everything. It makes heroes and villains of us all. And the choices we now need to make are really critical. Our decisions over the coming few years will determine whether we achieve our aspirations to become global citizens within a totally transformed, sustainable and compassionate system or whether the crushing force of current day economics, based on control and growth and the ignoring of external realities, lead aspiring citizens and nation states into a new dark age of serfdom or even slavery.

Bay Jordan has shone a bright light into this complex challenge and he simplifies and clarifies many of the issues in a very well-researched and entertaining way. He locates the main drivers and then drills down exposing how they underline, corrupt and corrode our vision of democracy.

This is a book that can be read as a simple narrative or as a masterful exposé of the democracy delusion.

The word democracy is a little bit like the word God. It has many different interpretations and people have their own idea of what democracy actually is. Bay dispenses with any confusion, diving deep into the etymology of the most transparent definition and starts by clarifying what "Governance of the people, for the people and by the people" actually means.

Not only does Bay articulate the nature of the threats with great erudition, he also proposes a series of practical solutions in order to embark on the journey to alter course to a more secure and sustainable future.

As I said, some of the decisions we take over the next few years will determine very different future paths indeed. The growing power of corporations, the declining capacity of democratic governments to manage their own economies where capital can flow freely across borders, the excesses and self-interest of the banking sector and the introduction of

FOREWORD

TTIP to consolidate this path makes Bay's book timely and one that needs to be taken very seriously indeed.

History is littered with examples of people who did not heed the obvious warning signs and suffered greatly as a consequence. We are in a similar position now.

The Democracy Delusion is a wake-up call! Winston Churchill put it perfectly when he said, "The era of procrastination, of half-measures, of soothing and baffling expedients of delay is coming to a close. In its place we are entering a period of consequences."

Read this book, be informed and take action to influence your friends, family and community to do the same.

Lawrence Bloom, 14 July 2015 (Bastille Day!)
Lawrence Bloom sat on the executive committee of the Intercontinental Hotel Group where he ran their global real estate portfolio. He was subsequently invited by the World Economic Forum in Davos to chair their Global Agenda Council on Urban Management and more recently by the UNEP Green Economy Initiative to chair their Green Cities, Buildings and Transport Council. Lawrence is currently Secretary General of the Be Earth Foundation, a United Nations intergovernmental organisation in collaboration with ECOSOC.

PREFACE

Like most things in everyday human existence, habits can be good and bad. We treasure people for their "good" habits and belittle them for their "bad" ones. But have you ever stopped to think how endemic and pervasive habits actually are? Before you can do that, however, you have to stop and think what a habit actually is.

My common everyday dictionary defines habit simply as, "a settled or regular tendency or practice."[1] That, however, seems a little too simplistic and – intuitively knowing there is more to it than that – I felt compelled to dig deeper. A more comprehensive definition identified habit as, "a) a behaviour pattern acquired by frequent repetition or physiologic exposure that shows itself in regularity or increased facility of performance; b) an acquired mode of behaviour that has become nearly or completely involuntary.[2] This certainly throws more light on the subject and is much more informative. Even this, though, only implies the psychological and physiological importance of habits, which are effectively a process whereby thinking moves from the conscious to the subconscious. So, for our purposes, let us work with the simple idea of a habit as "an ingrained or sub-conscious or irresistible behaviour."[3]

This not only makes habits personal, but it also means that they can often be unrecognised. And if they are unrecognised there is a strong likelihood that they are never challenged. Even if they are recognised, they may still never be questioned or challenged. This can be a problem, even with

---

[1] Reader's Digest Wordpower Dictionary.
[2] Merriam-Webster at http://www.merriam-webster.com/dictionary/habit
[3] The connection between habit and inhabit is also an interesting one. According to Merriam-Webster, the root of the word "habit" is the Latin "habere: to have, hold or possess" whereas the root of the word "inhabit" is the concatenation of the Latin words "in" and "habitare: to dwell." Thus you could say that we are possessed by habits or that habits dwell in us; either way there is a sense of permanency.

"good" habits, because as circumstances change so unconscious behaviour may no longer be appropriate and therefore, by definition, become a "bad" habit.

Restorers, collectors and connoisseurs are often amazed when they clean and restore old masterpieces and ancient artefacts. New techniques, details and discoveries delight, giving a renewed and deeper appreciation as they open up new insights that enhance knowledge, settle old debates or create new ones, and open up new channels of inquiry and investigation. In many ways this can be an analogy for life. Just as the passage of time with its fading, accumulated dust and dirt and inevitable wear and tear changes the original appearance and distorts and defaces ancient relics, so too with habits.

Victor Hugo once said, *"Habit is the nursery of errors."* Wise words, they clearly imply a need to consistently evaluate our habits. This is especially important if they are collective habits.

You may question that last statement. After all, we have just established that habits are personal, so how would it be possible to have a collective habit?

If you adhere strictly to our definition above, it may technically not be possible to have a collective habit. Nonetheless, a habit is first and foremost a pattern of behaviour, so you have to concede that the concept of collective behaviour is by no means far-fetched. You have only to think of a lynch mob or a "mob-mentality" to know that group human behaviour can be readily instigated. Thus, the key question then becomes, is it possible that group behaviour can be similarly governed by the sub-conscious? If so, then there is such a thing as a group habit.

And I would go so far as to say that, not only do group habits exist, but they are also more prevalent than you think. In fact I would define "conventional wisdom" as a group habit. Thus the prevalent theme of *The Democracy Delusion* is to illustrate just how pervasive and pernicious conventional wisdom is and how much damage it can wreak – and, in the context of democracy, it has wreaked – and to challenge some of the unchallenged thinking that underpins it, show its flaws, and to provide some suggestions as to how they can be redressed and not be allowed to become so dominant and destructive in the future.

Thus the book starts with the premise of "upside down" democracy, illustrating how the increasing dominance of central government destroys the very essence of democracy by making the thread between the electorate and government ever weaker. The dilution of accountability removes us further and further away from the original rallying cry of "liberty, fraternity and equality" and the concept of democracy as "government of the people, by the people, for the people." With increased power the driving force behind most government has become the attainment and retention of power – a considerable distance removed from being "for the people."

This narrow focus has either directly contributed to, or – at best – passively allowed, the economic disenfranchisement of the masses, evidenced by the increasing gaps in income and wealth. This is directly contrary to the underlying principles of democracy, and the equity that underpins it, and is prima facie evidence of the fact that democracy is failing.

This is enabled by "awful accounting" which exaggerates the apparent differences between the different types of entity and over-emphasises "profit" at the expense of value, thereby creating a dichotomy between "commercial" and "economic" principles which is a fundamental factor in "boom and bust" cycles. Apart from anything else, in economic downturns, this results in organisations offloading their costs onto the wider community and thereby exacerbating the cycle and causing even bigger peaks and troughs.

All this is facilitated by a legal and overly complex taxation system which permits, and even encourages, behaviour that not only plunders the economy but which also actively undermines its long-term viability, with behaviour at Barclays Bank used as an example to illustrate the point and underscore, again, the lack of basic economic understanding that seems to characterise business today.

It would seem that government is powerless to take meaningful action to prevent this, not least because election and re-election so often depends on contributions from the beneficiaries of that very system. This is exacerbated by the party political system and their dominance of the political scene, with policies being identified, designed and developed by a select group and then, after a party conference with much lobbying and behind the scenes negotiations, being approved by those members present to represent the party as a whole, becoming a binding commitment. This resultant manifesto then shapes all "party" behaviour for the duration of the next term of government and prevents any spontaneous, or possibly more appropriate, responses to changing situations and circumstances.

Thomas Jefferson pointed out that "democracy demands an educated and informed electorate" but our education systems are failing in this task too. Nowhere is this perhaps more apparent than in the riotous reactions to the economic turmoil in some of the Eurozone economies. This is manifest evidence of an electorate who do not understand enough about basic economics to understand the necessity for the actions being taken, or to have prevented it reaching such a state of affairs in the first place. The increased distance between voters and their representatives has perhaps exacerbated this and the ever-increasing sense of powerlessness by the voters may be evidenced in the declining turnouts at the polls.

Returning to the topic of the widening income and wealth gaps, you can see how these have been enabled by the manner in which the diseconomies of scale have been ignored. This is perfectly illustrated in the example of one of the world's premier companies where, regardless of the investments made over a 10 year period, the entire increase in profits can be accounted for by the savings in staff costs and the reduction of 110,000 people in that time. In other words, the entire increase in profits has been made at the expense of its people. What further proof do you need of the dichotomy between commercial and economic interests? If nothing else, this helps to explain the near record profit levels that are running concurrently with extremely high levels of unemployment.

While this is in itself a social time-bomb, the situation is compounded by what Woodrow Wilson described as "the invisible hand ... set up above the forms of democracy." This actually sabotages the state and makes social unrest almost inevitable at some time in the future. Key factors in this sabotage are:

- The corporate downsizing depicted in the above example;
- Tax avoidance
- Off-shoring

Governments depend to an enormous extent on the revenues from corporate taxes received from mega-corporations. The industrial scale tax avoidance by these companies thus deprive them of an enormous contribution. This compels government to look elsewhere, which inevitably results in the average citizen – the very people whose interests they are supposed to be looking out for – having to pay more tax, and therefore suffer a reduced standard of living.

Off-shoring, by moving jobs to other countries, almost inevitably means fewer jobs for that country's own people, thereby adding to the national social problems.

Combine these 3 elements and you are priming a social time-bomb. The clock is already ticking and unless some sort of corrective action is taken, soon, it may be impossible to avoid a social uprising. Certainly there is no sign in this that democracy is fulfilling its ideals.

This might all sound rather depressing but it is natural to point out what is wrong before you can start putting forward solutions. Thus, you need not fear that this is yet another personal rant or diatribe against big government and big business. Rather they lay the groundwork for a rational case for a different approach. Collectively they point to an "emperor's new clothes" scenario. They indicate how the policies ostensibly being introduced to address these problems are not working and call into question whether they were ever intended to work. Thus, even if they don't indict the integrity of government initiatives, they do - very clearly – indicate that democracy, as it currently operates, is not working and that some of the underlying collective wisdom that underpins its operation need to be challenged and replaced.

The Democracy Delusion starts this process. Firstly it rises above policy and looks at some of the principles that underpin democracy and how these have perhaps been lost sight of. Then it builds on these to create some solutions which, while they would not guarantee perfect democracy (recognising that in all likelihood there is no such thing), would provide a framework for ensuring a more stable form in which the current bad habits could be eradicated and providing a mechanism that would, hopefully, prevent future systems from forming a conventional wisdom that is never unchallenged.

Very briefly these solutions include:

- A new accounting regimen that applies across all organisation types, and that makes employees more integral to their operations, thereby making them more democratic as well as spreading the economic understanding that is currently deficient, cementing the foundations for a more effective democracy.
- A new, single-rate tax system that removes the inherent inequality of a progressive tax system that is fundamentally undemocratic to begin with. Furthermore this new system would also recognise that it is ultimately the individual who bears the economic brunt of all taxes and so would dispense with any corporate taxes; compensating for these by distributing a greater share of the results of organisational performance improvement and taxing those.

- A "right-side-up democracy", whereby revenues are allocated at the local level with central government getting a percentage (rather than the other way round that happens at present.) Ideally that percentage would be fixed by the constitution and only capable of being changed by approval from the electorate.
- A new sustainability, whereby an organisation's on-going viability is recognised as important to the community and that its viability in turn depends on that of the community and the environment. This will ensure a mutual dependency that reinforces a cycle of sustainability that benefits all and optimises the economic as well as the social factors.

This gives you a reasonable overview of the contents of the book, but I invite you to read further to get a better understanding of the detail and how they all hang together to provide for a new democracy in which the delusions of the modern form are no longer an issue.

INTRODUCTION

"If everyone is thinking alike then somebody isn't thinking."

GENERAL GEORGE S PATTON

There is more than an element of truth in that statement. This makes any conventional wisdom extremely dangerous.

Wikipedia – that modern oracle and font of all wisdom and knowledge – defines conventional wisdom as: "the body of ideas or explanations generally accepted as true by the public or by experts in a field. Such ideas or explanations, though widely held, are unexamined. Unqualified societal discourse preserves the *status quo*."

Key here are the words; "accepted as true," "widely held," and "unexamined", together with the consequences. If things are not examined they are not challenged and there is nothing to stimulate change, which makes it inevitable that the *status quo* will persist. This is particularly dangerous when the things that "are accepted as true" actually are not. This can easily happen because sometimes such thinking simply passes its sell-by date and outlives its usefulness and sometimes the thinking is totally flawed, has been all along and we just haven't been smart enough to realise it.

The words "unqualified societal discourse" are particularly striking. Of course this is just a fancy way of saying unthinking discussion at a community level, but the point is, if the underlying "truths" are not valid, it means that the consequences are felt by society as a whole. This can be disastrous, whether that society is simply a local community or a larger, even global community.

Unfortunately I think we are at a point in history when we are experiencing just that – the crisis of conventional wisdom – when we are discovering that we have been conned, the fundamental principles of what we have accepted as true are actually unsound, and the consequences of our blind belief are now coming home to roost.

Our ability to meet this crisis and overcome these challenges depends therefore on how quickly we can open up our minds and unlearn this so-called knowledge, which has been misdirecting us for so long. Therein lies a massive problem, for there are no real signs yet that we are ready to challenge this fraudulent conventional wisdom.

You will naturally challenge that statement. I know if I were you I would be asking myself, "How can he say that?" However, I ask you to just think about it for a moment. Think about everything that has happened since the 2008 financial crisis, yet how much has actually changed in the years since 2008? Rather like the First World War, which has been held up as an example of something that should never be allowed to happen again.

Even worse, think of the primary (not necessarily root) causes for that financial crisis – unsustainable borrowing. This meant that it was the first economic recession where the traditional remedy was not really viable, because it was not a practical proposition for governments to spend their way back to prosperity; spending more in a time of naturally declining national revenue would inevitably necessitate increased borrowing. In any crisis caused by a particular pattern of behaviour, it is simply insane to expect that more of such behaviour will lead you out of the crisis, and this possibly applies to an even greater extent in this financial situation. It was Einstein who said that you cannot solve a problem with the thinking that created it, and that applies here too, even though there appears to have been little thinking in the first place! Yet national approaches seem to bounce between policies demanding greater austerity and those calling for greater expenditure, notwithstanding the debt implications and the future ramifications of such action. What is this if not a rigid adherence to the conventional wisdom that this is the only way out of economic recession? It is hardly any wonder that national economies tend to be flat-lining or worse!

Despite this, people as a whole still keep hoping for a return to "the good times", when things go back to what they were before, and leaders and governments continue to encourage these hopes. Meanwhile the dearth of new ideas delivers a deafening, depressing silence and the longer this vacuum persists the longer the tough times will endure and the more difficult they will ultimately be. Nobody, however, appears to have the courage to say anything; possibly because they have convinced themselves that to say anything would lead to a self-fulfilling prophecy.

I don't know about you but, more than anything, I find this lack of innovation infuriating. I desperately want to see evidence of new ideas being put forward and debated and, where appropriate, trialled. It is with that hope in mind that I write this book, which continues my efforts to spark fresh thinking.

In the introduction to *A Feeling of Worth* I wrote about the mental struggle that I had faced in publishing my ideas: the conflict between following Reinhold Niebuhr's prayer to have, "the strength to change the things I can, the serenity to accept the things I cannot and the wisdom to know the difference" and recognising that this was an area where I could change things, along with the sense that somebody has to make change happen and that I was as much "somebody" as anybody. Eventually the realisation came that life must have a purpose and that I might not be fulfilling mine if I remained silent, which overcame my scruples and compelled me to write. Well it is even harder this time, not least because my earlier effort, unfortunately, did not have the effect I had hoped.

Perhaps I severely lack the serenity and wisdom that Niebuhr prayed for and should simply pray for more myself. However, I still cannot accept either the way things are or the possibility that I cannot make a contribution to changing them. So that just leaves me with the challenge of trying again and finding out whether I *do* have the strength to help facilitate change.

INTRODUCTION

Of course the truth is that my frustration with the *status quo* leaves me feeling far from serene, which makes it a little easier. That is, however, offset by the fact I am only too well aware that it is a fool that thinks he is a wise man and that by so expressing myself I run the risk of appearing to think myself wise yet prove myself a fool. But I don't honestly know whether it *is* wisdom to stay silent either. Consequently I feel I must press on and at least hope for some satisfaction from having tried. I also hope for some credit for my courage (or foolhardiness) for, having overcome this inner conflict once before, I find the struggle even harder this time. I simply try to find solace in the words of Confucius, "Yen Hui did not help me to think – he was a 'yes' man." I guess I can't be a "yes" man.

Furthermore, the challenge is made even greater by the fact that I am basically writing about the same issues that impelled *A Feeling of Worth*. Consequently I have to avoid repeating myself while making a clearer, more cogent and more convincing case – no small task!

The principle theme of *A Feeling of Worth* is that somehow our current systems have distorted values to such an extent that there is a decline in our sense of our self-worth. I attempted to show how this had come about, paradoxically through an over-emphasis of personal rights without a counter-balancing recognition of personal obligations to society and the world at large, and to put forward some practical ideas as to how this could be redressed. Since then nothing much has changed; the problems persist and there are few signs of any other solutions that offer hope of any meaningful change. We continue to lurch on – I would like to say forwards, but I don't think we can even be certain of the direction in which we are heading; sometimes it appears that we are actually going backwards or at least in circles. Unfortunately, this is not sustainable and if I were you I would be asking myself how we can turn things around, before disaster strikes and we end up in an even worse mess.

Naturally, I have been asking myself why it is so hard to spread new ideas and for them to take root. I have come up with two main answers.

The first is actually the corollary to Niebuhr's statement that you have to be in a position to make change. You cannot be 'somebody'; you have to be 'SOMEBODY.' In other words you have to have either a position of prestige or authority, or you have to have credibility through reputation and past achievements. This makes it very difficult for someone like me, who is forging a path in new territory. Even in this age of instant communication it isn't just a case of putting up a video and having it go viral. That may work when you are reaching out to a consumer audience, but it doesn't work when you are trying to reach world leaders and senior executives.

Of course you will not be surprised to learn that the second is conventional wisdom. This is a powerful force that creates habits, unthinking responses and knee-jerk reactions that – as we have seen – perpetuate the *status quo* and makes change incredibly difficult.

There is not much I can do about the former (although it would be great if you could help me take the message viral and ensure that we bring it before the people who can actually start to make it happen.) So I am focussing my attention on the latter and using this book to illustrate just how this phenomenon is conning us, holding us back and impeding progress, as a result of some "accepted truths" that are anything but true.

Accordingly, I repeat something I wrote in the introduction to *A Feeling of Worth*.

> "The fact is that Niebuhr was wrong. It was Einstein who said, "The world is a dangerous place; not because of the people who are evil, but because of the people who don't do anything about it." We are all in this world together and as such we have joint responsibility for what happens. As soon as we accept that there are some human activities which we cannot influence and just leave to others, we find they get hi-

jacked and become corrupt and dangerous, and ultimately put everything we believe in at risk. At the same time, it destroys our own feeling of worth."

With that thought I invite you to open up your mind and come along as I take you on a journey that looks at the way in which some examples of conventional wisdom may actually be sabotaging the very goals they are supposed to be addressing. I ask you to go further and see if you can come up with more of your own. Then I ask you to review the principles that underpin the solutions I am putting forward, and see if there is anything there, with which you can take issue. If there isn't – and I would be surprised if there was – then I ask you to review the solutions that I am putting forward and consider whether they are worth championing. If you feel they are, then please do whatever you can in your own environment to champion them so, together, we can make a difference, enable a better future and help make the world a better place.

PART ONE
MISPLACED CONVENTIONS

CHAPTER ONE
UPSIDE-DOWN DEMOCRACY

> "Remember, democracy never lasts long. It soon wastes, exhausts and murders itself. There never was a democracy yet that did not commit suicide."
>
> **JOHN ADAMS**

The ideal of democracy may be the greatest example of conventional wisdom. Notwithstanding the call by Adams and others to continually challenge our thinking about democracy, it would seem that we have signally failed to do so. As a result, it occupies a unique place in the world where we virtually idolise it. Those of us who believe we have it tend to take it for granted – so much so that we do very little to safeguard it, despite a lot of talk. This while those of us who don't have it aspire to it and die to acquire it.

Paradoxically, even as such struggles persist in many parts of the world, democracy itself is in jeopardy and I fear that Adams' words may yet prove prophetic. However, before we can assess the threat and how to fight it, we need to take a fresh look at what it is.

REVISION – WHAT IS DEMOCRACY?

> "Government of the people, by the people, for the people."
>
> **ABRAHAM LINCOLN**

Lincoln's definition remains perhaps one of the best known definitions of democracy. It may also be one of the most succinct. However, it doesn't give any indications of how to carry it out. This is perhaps unfortunate, because it its universal, all-inclusive nature makes it by far the most difficult form of government.

It certainly is not a logical choice, which you can perhaps deduce from the fact that the classical democracies of Greece and Rome had their origins in the reaction to abuse resulting from the concentration of power in the hands of individuals. The development of democracy in the 17th and 18th centuries mirrored that reaction.

If even democratic government is not ideal we should perhaps start by asking ourselves the most basic of all questions: why do we need a government in the first place?

ANARCHY

That question may not be as dumb as it first appears. Despite its more populist definition as a term for chaos, my dictionary defines anarchy as: "a system of government founded on the principles of anarchism." (Don't you just hate it when dictionaries use a variation of the same word to define it?) However, when you scan upwards you see that it defines anarchism as: "belief in the abolition of all government and the organisation of society on a co-operative basis." Thus the Hollywood depiction of anarchists as the original terrorist plotters would seem to be an extreme exaggeration. Anarchy would, on the surface at least, appear to be a legitimate form of alternative government.

The fact, however, that there is no known anarchist state in the world suggests that it is not a very practical concept. This is reinforced by a lack of any historical precedent. (Could it possibly be that true democracy is the closest approximation that we have?)

Before leaving the subject, however, it is worthwhile probing the term government and what it actually conveys. A combined definition (since my trusty dictionary commits the same offence here!) depicts it as: "the system by which a state or community manages the policy and affairs of its subjects."

Perhaps key here is the word "system" and since even a cooperative approach would demand some sort of system it would seem that anarchy is not a lack of government but *is* an alternative form of government.

Considering government as a system also gives us a useful basis to assess democracy. So let us now return to Lincoln's definition, taking each element in turn.

GOVERNMENT OF THE PEOPLE

This term has a dual meaning. Firstly, it represents the possessive case and thus conveys the ideal of the people metaphorically "owning" the government. This "ownership" is thus used to convey the message that the people's government is ultimately responsible to its people.

It is perhaps more important, however, to look at it from the sense of the people being governed. This distinguishes it from the other forms of government because it breaks from the traditional perspective of regarding the people as "subjects." Instead, it makes government the servant because you now have a government whose primary responsibility is the welfare of the people.

This is significant for it establishes a very basic principle: namely that people matter. Now not only is it a people's government, but it is responsible for their well-being. This is definitely unique, for even though other forms may embrace the concept, this is more likely to be from a paternalistic perspective or a self-interest perspective. Democracy is unique in making government a calling rather than a right.

GOVERNMENT BY THE PEOPLE

This is also significant. Now the people are responsible for running the system. This takes the fact that they are no longer subjects to the next level. It means that they are no longer the victims of the actions others, but are responsible for their own fate. This, however, does not give them the right to only look after their own interests. It creates a mutual dependency that links their self-interest inextricably with the interests of their fellow citizens.

So here too is another basic principle that pervades every aspect of democratic life.

GOVERNMENT FOR THE PEOPLE

At first glance there seems to be nothing particularly noteworthy about this. It simply serves to reinforce both the previous principles. It takes their implied duties and makes them clear and makes them explicit. Yet, on further reflection it is no less important. It brings everything into focus and gives it all a purpose.

Purpose is essential because it creates power. Purpose unites and thereby not only creates energy, enthusiasm and engagement, but it also counters drift. This is vital because drift is the child of conventional wisdom and inevitably results in apathy and ultimately leads to chaos. However, the key here is that the focus of the purpose is on the wider good: the minute it shifts to self-interest the foundations of democracy start to crumble.

THE SIGNIFICANCE OF THIS

You may well be asking yourself why this is important. It is important because it takes us back to the essence of democratic government.

All too often today we hear about "back to basics" initiatives. Unfortunately their success rate is nothing like as good as it could be – or should be. Possibly the main reason for this is that they don't go far enough back to challenge the ingrained conventional wisdom. If you really want to get to basics you have to go back to the very essence of what you are trying to do and the only way to do that is to go back to the underlying principles.

The rallying cry

"LIBERTÉ, ÉGALITÉ, FRATERNITÉ!"

"Liberty, equality, fraternity!" is the phrase that fuelled the French Revolution. Or so history tells us. But, even if the accuracy of that claim is open to debate, it still makes a wonderful slogan or mission statement. And it has certainly come to represent the ideal of democracy. As a result it is a very good launching pad for an assessment of modern democracy and where we stand in relation to its ideals.

What is the difference between an ideal and a principle? There is none really, for a dictionary defines ideal in part as, "A principle to be aimed for, a standard of perfection." So you could say that each of the three elements is a basic principle. Thus they certainly present a good place to continue our principle-based review and the ideal starting point for a fresh assessment of democratic government and how it is performing against these original values. Let's look at each in turn.

LIBERTY

In a modern world we may find this one a little strange. After all, particularly for those of us in the western world, liberty is something that we pretty much take for granted. Yet at the time of the French Revolution slavery was possibly at its peak. And even those who were not slaves were still hardly much better off. Remember the infamous phrase that lit the fuse? "Let them eat cake." While once again history actually challenges the attribution of those words to Marie Antoinette, they nevertheless appear to have been highly inflammatory, and that could only have been the case if the people perceived an injustice.

One of the great ironies of life is that perceptions govern emotions, and hence actions, far more than facts. So it doesn't really matter whether the story is true. What does matter is that the people did not feel free. They felt powerless and inferior and resented the fact that others were in control of their destiny. So they revolted.

The uprisings of the Arab Spring in 2011 suggest that there are still people who feel like that. Clearly then liberty is still not universal. But, even more frightening, is the fact you find people who do not feel free even in countries where you would take freedom for granted. How else do you explain the fertile ground in which terrorist ideals spread within the "free" countries of the west – the so-called "home-grown terrorists"? Like Hamlet they remain prisoners of their thinking. And, paradoxically, rather than recognising and valuing the freedom that enables them to plan their atrocities, they scorn it as weakness.

Of course there are different types of freedom. Possibly one that matters most is the freedom of choice; something that we in the "developed world" have come to take for granted. As we have become progressively more affluent, it has become one of the manifestations of that affluence. We have been able to choose what we do, and when, where and how we do it. This freedom of choice – implicitly recognised in the phrase "life-style choice" – has extended to cover our work, our leisure, our consumption, our behaviour and our environment. With the threat to economic stability and declining standards of living, however, these can no longer be taken for granted as they have been. The loss of something you had previously and no longer have is a greater source of dissatisfaction than not having it in the first place.

Consequently, you could say that we are experiencing a loss of liberty. We now have to think about things that previously we didn't. While that of itself may not be a bad thing, the very fact of having to do so can be perceived as a constraint and thus, by definition, a loss of liberty and cause for discontent. And, as the French aristocracy learned the hard way, discontent can breed trouble.

EQUALITY

Very closely aligned with this perceived lack of freedom is the sense of inequality.

The French philosophers saw liberty and equality as the two constant essentials of democracy. They often used justice, safety, and property alongside or instead of fraternity, but they never dropped liberty and equality. And they always saw the two as inextricably linked.

Of course that makes sense. Nothing invokes a sense of injustice more readily than a feeling of inequality. And nothing compounds a sense of inequality more than an inability to do anything about it. We probably could all complain that life isn't fair, but for the most part we can accept that as a fact of life. There are times, however, when the apparent injustice of things eats away at us and turns into resentment. Resentment is never healthy and it can also be extremely contagious. When it is, you have the seeds of revolt. Inequality transcends the boundaries of reason and starts breeding resentment when you feel powerless to change anything. And you feel powerless when you don't have the freedom to do what you think you need or want to do.

Now of course equality per se is an impossible ideal. People are not the same and that alone means that things are not, and never will be, equal. On top of that situations are invariably the consequence of choice. Different choices lead to different outcomes. That inevitably creates inequality. Most people recognise this and accept it. Thus inequality only becomes a problem when the differences become disproportionate or unreasonable, the latter, for example, when people take advantage of position or influence to take away something that we feel is important, or to gain something valuable for themselves.

Unfortunately, as we shall see later, the ever-widening gap between rich and poor suggests that this is the case. So equality will become an issue. Declining livings standards are always a problem, but when they are exacerbated by a sense of powerlessness, people lose their sense of freedom too. They see themselves as victims. That is what is happening in western economies, which, of course, creates the potential for a new revolution, as the people try to restore the democracy that they believe has failed.

FRATERNITY

Liberty and equality then are clearly essential ingredients of democracy, and very closely linked. They are, however, by no means the only ingredients, and fraternity is widely considered as the third. Although this may not have been quite so obvious or so vociferously proclaimed since democracy became more established, it is no less important for all that.

Anthropology teaches us that man cannot survive on his own. The logical extension of this is that success is never dependent on the individual alone. So at its most basic the concept of brotherhood is simply a natural acknowledgement of that. It implies a kinship that creates a sense that "we are all in this together." Of course this makes even more sense when you link it with equality, because it reinforces the sense of mutual dependency – with no meritocracy. It removes any judgment call and creates a moral obligation.

Unfortunately, it is another area where we don't seem to be doing too well. Whether you regard it as a realistic measure or not, a key indicator of the brotherhood of man is social mobility, and it seems as this is in decline in most of the established democracies, particularly in the UK and US. The growing inequality is exacerbated by a shrinking middle class that appears to be being squeezed by a growing underclass and an increasing gap with the wealthy. As I shall demonstrate later, this appears to be because the middle class seems to be funding both, at the cost of its own well-being.

A UTOPIAN VISION?

When you consider the three elements in this light, they certainly do present a challenge. But when you acknowledge an ideal as a "standard for perfection" that is hardly surprising.

The questions you then instinctively ask yourself are, "Does this mean we are asking for Utopia? Are we aiming for the impossible?"

Margaret Thatcher once said, "Politics in its purest form is philosophy in action." There doesn't seem to be much evidence these days of "pure politics" but if you take philosophy to mean "a theory or attitude to guide one's behaviour" she might have had a point. That implies, however, a potential for division or conflict according to different personal "theories or attitudes." Such potential can only be reduced by returning to and continually drilling down to principles or ideals.

There is no question that democracy creates high expectations and as a result it places a heavy burden on us. That does not mean, however, that we should see it as an impossible mission. Rather it presents us with a great challenge. Too often we see perfection as an impossible goal and consequently we give up before we have even begun. The problem with that – with seeing ideals as an unattainable goal – is that you start to scoff at them. This leads to a lowering of standards and an inevitable decline in behaviour. As the old bumper sticker had it, "It is difficult to soar like an eagle when you are flying with turkeys." Similarly, it is hard to attain high standards if you don't set high goals, and for that reason ideals are essential. This is another reason why – if ideals and principles are synonymous terms – we need to begin with principles.

Maybe this is easier to understand when you look at it from a different perspective. So let us now return to government and how all this fits in with the democratic government that Lincoln depicted.

Back to government

It seems appropriate to begin by asking ourselves how close to true democracy our present systems of government are. How well are they doing at embracing and adhering to the three principles of liberty, equality and fraternity? You might think that they are doing well but, as I have hinted, this may not be the case.

Arguably, government today has completely lost sight of these principles. It would certainly seem to be *of* the people, (at least in the second sense noted above) but the extent to which it is *by* the people is debatable and the extent to which it is *for* the people is extremely doubtful. Let's take a closer look.

THE GREAT CHALLENGE

To get to grips with these issues you have to begin with the most basic question – who are "the people"? It is easy to understand what the term means when you are talking about the "of". The idea of a population at large presents no problems when you refer to the governed. The need for order and a system of guiding rules and regulations to shape behaviour is self-evident and thus the generic term "people" presents no problems at all, because it is all-inclusive; its universality happily accommodates everyone because there is no need to distinguish anyone. Basically if conforms to the ideal of equality.

This is not the case, however, when selecting the people to do the governing – those who form the "by." The sheer numbers involved make it impossible for the general term to apply here. Thus there is a need to select representatives from the population to whom this aspect can be delegated. Inevitably this tends to "make some people more equal than others" and so makes matters much more subjective and thus, equally inevitably, more controversial. It brings us back to the question of democracy being an impossible ideal.

Historically we haven't done too badly at devising ways to address this problem, based on two universal principles:

- A universal franchise; and
- The accountability of the elected, with the electorate having the right to replace them if they are dissatisfied.

Ignoring for now some of the practical problems around the election process itself (which I will deal with later) these still do not provide the panacea that we might hope. The reason for that is that we have somehow inverted democracy.

The reality is, in order to ensure that it is effective, democracy requires people to be involved. Yet somehow we have all got less involved; we tend to feel increasingly powerless and that our participation is futile and our vote meaningless. That is because the power to make the decisions that matter lies increasingly at national government or even higher level. This makes us feel further and further removed and weakens our faith in the accountability of those whom we have elected. This creates a negative spiral that makes us feel more despondent and irrelevant and consequently we become increasingly apathetic. That spiral means things only get worse, and – because they start feeling invincible – those doing the governing start to become more self-serving, forgetting the reasons they were elected, if not the people they are representing. Making a statement in a manifesto is all very fine when votes are at stake, but suddenly the issue becomes less important and the challenges more daunting once the votes have been secured and power is assured for a few years.

That is what I mean by "upside down" democracy. In order to have a more effective democracy it has to start closer to home[4], for the more remote you are from the "by" the more susceptible to corruption the "for" part of democracy gets. You saw some evidence of this earlier, when we looked at the widening wealth gap. You would agree that is hardly compatible with government for the people, especially when equality is one of the fundamental elements of democracy. Well, it gets worse.

---

[4] I will deal with this more later, but I have already spelled out how we could reverse this in "A Feeling of Worth."

SELFISH GOVERNMENT

A major consequence of this centralisation of government is that government itself has become too powerful. Indeed it has mushroomed to such an extent that it has become the end rather than the means.

In fact you could even go so far as to say that government has virtually become an industry all on its own. Its reach extends further and further into everyday life. This is inevitable for its self-perpetuation means the number of laws promulgated proliferates profusely. Of course the unavoidable consequence of this is that more and more laws get broken. Which is why you should not be surprised that prison populations are growing! When thinking about this, please remember that the first, second, third, fourth and fifth priorities of any bureaucracy are all concerned with its own survival. Don't expect any bureaucracy to do anything that does not result, directly or indirectly, in more bureaucratic jobs. Whether or not the things they do add value to "the people" is beside the point – they add value to the bureaucracy.

It also means that the government, directly or indirectly, employs more and more people. Thus it consumes an ever increasing proportion of national GDP. So much so that its purchasing power can distort industries and even entire economies, and, perhaps more disturbingly, means we become more and more dependent on government. After all if you took this to an extreme what would happen when the government grew to employ everyone? As the only taxpayers left, public sector employees would have to pay tax at a 100% rate. In other words you would effectively return to a state of slavery. While that may be "riding the curve of extrapolation to cloud cuckoo land," it does indicate how dangerous, debilitating and destructive the growth of government can be.

There are two clear indicators of this. Firstly, just listen to the radio and television and see how every time there is a problem government is expected to sort it out. Horse meat in the beef? It's a government problem! Increasing food prices? The government must do something! Rising energy bills – the government needs to regulate the utility companies more! And possibly the worst example of all: government is expected to generate economic growth.

The problem with this attitude is that it leads to increased government spending. Even more disturbingly this growth in government consumption has also led to the massive increase in government borrowings, to the extent that there is hardly a government in the world today that is not massively in debt. The national debt of virtually every single democratic country is the second clear sign of this unhealthy dependence on government. This excessive borrowing is one of the primary reasons for the economic crisis that overshadows the entire European economy and the global financial markets and is what makes finding a solution such a challenge.

When you are up to your eye-balls in debt you cannot borrow more money simply to pay off your debts. Just as you don't want more rain during a flood, you don't want or need more debt when you are struggling to pay off existing debt! Unfortunately though, governments are finding that, even as they try to pay off the existing debt, they need to keep borrowing more. Even more frightening is the fact that there are so many who still believe that the way out of the crisis is to increase spending; further evidence of the disastrous drag of conventional wisdom.[5]

Few, other than academics and so-called radicals, question the *raison d'etre* for government, yet it is only by re-examining the purpose of government that you can define its role and how it should be shaped. It is only by re-examining the role of government that you can create a proper framework for government, with the checks and balances to ensure

---

[5] I also highlighted this growing dependence on government and the issues of its cost and sustainability in "A Feeling of Worth". Since then, however, we have witnessed the consequences in the collapse or near-collapse of several indebted countries and the threat this has posed to the Eurozone and global economies.

that it does not become too powerful or too cumbersome or too ineffective.

Hopefully, since necessity is the mother of invention, more people will start to do so now and this crisis will provide the launching pad for redefining, reshaping and remodelling government. There is no getting away from the need for government of some sort, but if it is to be of the people, by the people and for the people we need to ensure that we align it accordingly and equip it to do its job properly and effectively.

Let's not forget that we are the ones who have to make democracy work. After all as Aung San Suu Kyi has said, "Democracy is when people keep the government in check." We will look at more reasons why this is necessary later.

CHAPTER TWO
THE EROSION OF EQUALITY

> "There are three kinds of lies: lies, damned lies and statistics."
>
> **BENJAMIN DISRAELI**

We are all familiar with Disraeli's statement, even if we were not aware that it was he who first said it, but nowhere is this more true than when it comes to measuring wealth. After all wealth is not an absolute. Rather it is a derived number that depends on a plethora of variables. This makes it a statistic that is in turn dependent on other statistics. Let's have a closer look at this to see what I am saying.

WHAT IS WEALTH?

Wealth is the colloquial term for 'net worth.' And the definition of net worth is "the sum of all assets minus the sum of all liabilities" or – to put it more simply – "the difference between what you own and what you owe." It is thus a simple arithmetic formula that can be written as follows:

$$\text{Wealth (W)} = \text{Assets (A)} - \text{Liabilities (L)}$$

Now that's all very well and good, but the values of A and L might not be the same on consecutive days. Thus your wealth is never constant but can, and does, vary from day to day. Thus it is rather silly to be hung up on your wealth at any particular time, because the only time it really matters is the day you die, when all your assets and liabilities are liquidated and their final value determined. Then and only then is your true wealth determined, and even then it can depend on whether you had the fortune to die at a good time or at a bad time relative to their value. And by that time it doesn't really affect you anyway although it might make a major difference to the goodwill with which you are sent on your way by your fortunate or unfortunate heirs!

Let's take a simplistic hypothetical example to illustrate this.

Dan Dead dies on the 31st July and his estate is wound up with the following assets and liabilities including shares that at the time of his death were worth 15.00 each.

	Assets	Liabilities	Net Worth
House	250,000		
Car	20,000		
10,000 Shares in XYZ Corporation	150,000		
Bank Balance	2,000		
Personal Belongings	1,000		
Mortgage Outstanding		100,000	
Personal Loans		15,000	
TOTAL	423,000	115,000	308,000

Donna Dyer by some strange coincidence has exactly the same assets and liabilities but dies on the 1st August after a collapse in the stock market – not as a result Dan Dead's death but following further major market concerns about growing government debt and the Eurozone crisis. As a result shares in XYZ had declined by 50% and were now valued at only 7.50. Her net worth thus looks like this:

	Assets	Liabilities	Net Worth
House	250,000		
Car	20,000		
10,000 Shares in XYZ Inc.	75,000		
Bank Balance	2,000		
Personal Belongings	1,000		
Mortgage Outstanding		100,000	
Personal Loans		15,000	
TOTAL	348,000	115,000	233,000

In the words of the old song, "What a difference a day makes!"

WHY WEALTH IS IMPORTANT

With wealth being so transient, inconstant and inconsistent you could argue that it is hardly an appropriate measure for measuring well-being, and even less appropriate for assessing the effectiveness of equality. Nevertheless I shall do so, for several reasons:

- Firstly, while wealth may be almost phantasmagorical by nature it is nevertheless largely a determinant of our standard of living and thus the material quality of our existence;
- Secondly, by nature and common usage, wealth is more of a comparative measure than an empirical one. Thus it matters not so much for its own sake but, through what it brings us, as a broad measure of our relative status in society. This may to some extent also be attributable to the fact that wealth is often confused with a high disposable income which, if the recipient is not too extravagant, means that you don't have to dip into assets to maintain living standards. Hence wealth is also easier to maintain because low disposable income can lead to wealth erosion.
- Lastly, because there are no other feasible alternatives. Despite its ethereal nature, wealth is one of the few common measures, if not the only one, that we have for assessing individual and collective well-being.

Despite this, you may still be wondering what all this has to do with democracy and/or the principles that underpin it. So let me explain.

It is possible to claim that democracy has underpinned the economic development that the world has seen over the past 200-240 years. This assumption underpins everything in this book and, while I believe it is well-founded, I feel it is incumbent on me to explain why. Thus, while I think it is fairly obvious that this prosperity began with the Industrial Revolution and that most people would accept this fact without any quibble, I don't want to be guilty of the kind of conventional wisdom or unthinking acceptance of facts that I am criticising. So we need some evidence to substantiate the claim.

The chart[6] below by the acclaimed economist, Angus Maddison does that. It shows the astronomic growth in per capita GDP over the past 200 years. Apart from a growth curve of the kind that any CEO or Sales Manager would give their right hand to have, you can see that the massive and virtually continuous growth begins around the time of the Industrial Revolution. And, it is hardly coincidence that the Industrial Revolution itself corresponded with the rise of Western democracy. It, therefore, seems entirely logical to conclude that the growth that followed the Industrial Revolution resulted from the rise of democracy and that the two are inextricably linked. Indeed historians generally acknowledge this, and cite the democratic upsurge as one of the root causes of The Industrial Revolution.

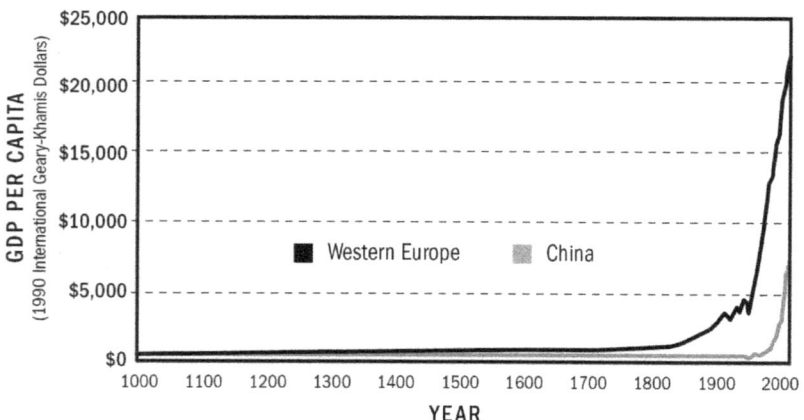

Some might argue that it was the other way around – that the industrial revolution could have been the driver for democracy. Certainly the two are linked, but in which direction does the causal link go? I personally think that the chart which

---

[6] Chart compiled using data from Angus Maddison's Historical Statistics of the World Economy 1- 2008 and reproduced in accordance with licence from Wikipedia

shows the rapid economic development in China – hardly the epitome of democracy – which seems to coincide broadly with the demise of Mao Tse Tung is evidence that democracy is the chicken and not the egg. It will be interesting to see to what extent China transforms over the coming years.

Of course if this belief in equality brought in the Industrial Age, then it follows that there would be an expectation that the rewards of this new prosperity should be spread. This growth in per capita GDP suggests that has been the case.

Yet while this new productivity created unprecedented prosperity and heralded wealth and well-being for many, the truth is that the distribution has never been equal or equitable. And this inequality has been at the heart of industrial relations disputes over the entire two hundred odd years since. Fortunately the widespread benefits and general sense of well-being this growth has engendered has, for the most part, ensured that dissatisfaction has been contained and never been allowed to get out of hand. Nevertheless that possibility remains and should the inequity reach unacceptable levels the danger of a new revolution always exists.

That is why the wealth gap and/or the earnings gap are important barometers of democratic performance. They are a crude measure of how well we are doing at creating equality and should thus be regarded as early warning indicators of potential problems. That is why I am concerned that current statistics show that we could be reaching the threshold of unacceptability. Unfortunately no-one knows precisely where that point is and so no-one can say how close to the red-line we are. But even so, these measures are sounding a warning that is not being heeded and that we ignore at our peril. (As I am sure the French nobility ignored those warnings presented to them prior to the French revolution. I would just prefer that we don't make the same mistake!)

In case you are not aware of them let me share some of the more specific, current warning signs with you.

ECONOMIC DISENFRANCHISEMENT

Undoubtedly the biggest single sign of the increasing failure of democracy is the increasing disparity of earnings and the widening wealth gap between the wealthy and the rest. These are in fact two distinct features of a massive subversive attack.

Disparity of Earnings

You may question this, but think for a moment about the basic underlying principles of democracy; liberty, equality and brotherhood. Of course it is a massive misrepresentation to think either that people are equal or that they can all be treated equally. Nevertheless the principle of equality does demand that everybody should be treated equitably and a widening income gap reverses the historic trend of democracy which has underpinned both the capitalist and socialist ideals and seen increasingly widespread prosperity across the board over the past two hundred years or more that we have just studied. This disparity, at the very least, demands an examination to see what has been happening for, as Louis D Brandeis has said, "We can have democracy in this country, or we can have great wealth concentrated in the hands of a few, but we can't have both."

The link between a sound economy and democracy may be tenuous, but there is no doubt that Maddison was correct. It exists and there is other historic precedent to demonstrate it. You only have to look back to 1914 when Henry Ford shocked the world by unilaterally introducing a minimum wage of $5 a day for his workers, more than double the industrial average of $2.34 a day. He explained his action by saying it "has the same effect as throwing a stone in a still pond by creating an ever-widening circle of buying that increases everyone's prosperity." However, his astuteness ran even deeper than that for he simultaneously reduced their working week from 6 days to 5 whilst setting a standard 8 hours per day shift. Ford saw that this was good for his own bottom line and the nation's too, for he understood:

- He could not earn great profits if people could not afford to buy his products.
- They would not want to buy his products if they did not have the leisure time to use them.

These are the fundamental principles that have underpinned Western industry and growth since the wars. Thus it would appear that a widening earnings gap is a threat to both our on-going economic well-being and to the ultimate health of our democracy. And you do not have to look too hard to understand why this is happening: the destabilising effect of performance related pay or incentive remuneration.

According to the Annual Survey of Hours and Earnings, produced by the UK Office of National Statistics, the average earnings in 2010 were £26,500 and the average bonus was £1,020. Simple arithmetic therefore tells us that the average pre-bonus earnings would have been £25,480 which means that the average bonus rate would have been 4%.

There are no readily available figures for middle managers, but let us assume that your average middle manager earns twice the average basic wage. That would be £50,960. Let us then assume that the manager gets a 10% bonus. His earnings would then increase to £56,056.

Now let us look at executive pay. According to Will Hutton[7] the remuneration for FTSE 100 Chief Executives in 2010 was eighty-eight times the UK median wage, up from forty-eight times, ten years earlier. According to my rudimentary calculations[8] that would make the average CEO pay packet £2,332,000. I have no idea of the breakdown of those figures but, based on news reports that the CEO of Lloyds TSB bank was getting a bonus of 225% on a salary of £1 million, let's create a little table.

---

[7] Source: Will Hutton Fair Pay Commission 2010, http://www.hm-treasury.gov.uk/press_hutton_interim.htm.
[8] Note: I have actually used the average rather than median for this calculation, thus ignoring the statistical differences. This means that my figures are conservative and the spread is likely to be wider than I am actually showing.

Let's be conservative and say then that the average base earnings for middle managers is double the average basic wage, at £50,960. And assume that the average CEO base salary was £1.1million and the average bonus rate was 112%. (Half that of the bank executive.) Then a table of earnings would look something like this:

LEVEL	BASE	BONUS %	BONUS	GROSS
EMPLOYEE	25,480	4	1,020	26,500
MIDDLE MANAGER	50,960	10	5,096	56,056
CHIEF EXECUTIVE	1,100,000	112	1,232,000	2,332,000

Now remember those averages include everyone in the workforce. That means they include the earnings of chief executives. Without those the averages for regular employees would be considerably less. Also remember that the higher bonus percentage is against an already large base. It is no wonder the earnings gap is widening to such an alarming extent. (It may also go a long way towards explaining why employee engagement is such an issue and, furthermore, one that is unlikely to go away until this earnings disparity is addressed.)

Although I have used UK figures to make the point, this is not a problem that is confined to the UK alone. The US has the same problem, for here it is estimated that 1% of the population earns 21% of the national income. As you will see shortly other OECD countries show similar trends albeit not to the same extent.

Now it does seem perverse to expect people to adhere to democratic principles in every aspect of life except their working lives. Even so calls for greater democracy in the workplace are not yet very widespread, although I am pleased to say that Traci Fenton is starting to make great headway on this through her Worldblu organisation.⁹ So at this stage prevailing attitudes appear acceptable, although once again it is a case of the prevailing conventional wisdom that is holding things back. Unfortunately, this is also undermining general democracy as we understand it.

The really bad news, however, is that the earnings gap is only half the story for, as you would expect, it leads to a widening wealth gap. And the wealth gap is widening even faster than the income gap.

Widening Wealth Gap

An Economic Policy Institute report dated 2011,[10] makes pretty gloomy reading. It states "The Great Recession officially lasted from December 2007 through June 2009 – the longest span of recession since the Great Depression. The recovery since then has proceeded on two tracks: one for typical families and workers, who continue to struggle against high rates of unemployment and continued foreclosures, and another track for the investor class and wealthy, who have enjoyed significant gains in the stock market and benefited from record corporate profits."

Key findings in this brief include:

- The destruction of wealth that resulted from the Great Recession was widespread but not uniform. From 2007 to 2009, average annualised household declines in wealth were 16% for the richest fifth of Americans and 25% for the remaining four-fifths.
- The divvying up of the total wealth pie, even as the pie shrank, was made more uneven due to larger drops in wealth for those at the bottom. The share of wealth held by the richest fifth of American households increased

---

[9] For further information about Traci and the principles of workplace democracy, as well as insight into some of the remarkable results that companies that espouse and follow her principles are achieving see http://www.worldblu.com

[10] EPI Briefing Paper "The State of Working America's Wealth, 2011: Through volatility and turmoil the gap widens" by Sylvia A Allegretto, March 23, 2011 Briefing Paper #292

by 2.2 percentage points to 87.2%, while the remaining four-fifths gave up those 2.2 percentage points and held onto just 12.8% of all wealth.
- The wealthiest 1% of U.S. households had net worth that was 225 times greater than the median or typical household's net worth in 2009. This is the highest ratio on record.
- In 2009, approximately one in four U.S. households had zero or negative net worth, up from 18.6% in 2007. For black households the figure was about 40%.
- The median net worth of black households was $2,200 in 2009, the lowest ever recorded; the median among white households was $97,900.
- Even at the 2007 economic peak, half of all U.S. households owned no stocks at all — either directly or indirectly through mutual or retirement funds.
- Home-ownership rates fell from a peak of 69.0% in 2004 to 67.2% in 2009, and house prices fell 32% from 2006 through the first quarter of 2009. Prices have since rebounded slightly but were at mid-2003 levels in the third quarter of 2010.
- Because of the housing bust, home equity as a percent of home value fell from 59.5% in the first quarter of 2006 to 36.2% in the fourth quarter of 2009. For the first time on record, the percent of home value that homeowners own outright dropped below 50% — meaning that banks now own more of the nation's housing stock than people do.

To me these figures are alarming and a real cause for concern. Particularly as they seem to point to an on-going deterioration unless some positive action is taken to reverse this. How can you explain (and, more importantly, justify) 13 million unemployed Americans at a time when corporations are making record profits? That has to be a pressure cooker and something has to blow.

You may be inclined to shrug this off by saying that it is just one country (even if it does happen to be the largest economy in the world.) But the US is not alone. The Occupy Wall Street campaign is a glaring consequence of this, but the fact that it has spread so widely across the world suggests that is not a national problem but a global one. The OECD chart[11] below shows the how the income gap we were looking at earlier has increased throughout the developed world in the past 20 years.

HUGE DIFFERENCES IN INCOME GAPS BETWEEN RICH AND POOR ACROSS OECD COUNTRIES

Levels of inequality in the latest year before the crisis and in the mid-1980s, working-age population

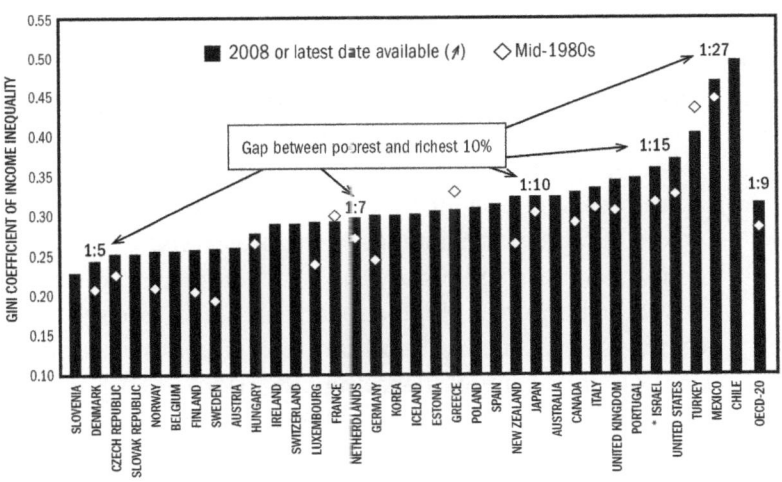

Note: The Gini coefficient ranges from 0 (perfect equality) to 1 (perfect inequality). Gaps between poorest and richest are the ratio of average income of the bottom 10% to average income of the top 10%. Income refers to disposable income adjusted for household size. * Information on data for Israel: http//dx.doi.org/10.1787/888932315602.
Source: OECD Income Distribution and Poverty Database (www.oecd.org/els/social/inequality)

---

[11] OECD report, "Divided We Stand: Why Inequality Keeps Rising." 19 December 2011

The report gives the following reasons for this:

- Significant income and earnings gains of higher-skilled technology workers compared to their less-skilled colleagues.
- Regulatory reforms and institutional changes increased employment opportunities but also contributed to greater wage inequality as a result of having more low-paid workers employed.
- Part-time work increased, atypical labour contracts became more common and the coverage of collective-bargaining arrangements declined in many countries;
- The rise in the supply of skilled workers helped offset the increase in wage inequality resulting from technological progress, regulatory reforms and institutional changes.
- Changing family structures make household incomes more diverse and reduce economies of scale. There are more single-headed households today than ever before; in working-age households, on average, in OECD countries. In couple households, employment rates of the wives of top earners increased the most. And in all countries, marriage behaviour has changed. People are now much more likely to choose partners in the same earnings bracket: so rather than marrying nurses, doctors are now increasingly marrying other doctors. Again, all of these factors contributed to higher inequality but much less so than the changes in the labour markets.
- The distribution of non-wage incomes has generally also become more unequal. In particular, capital income inequality increased more than earnings inequality in two-thirds of OECD countries.
- Tax and benefit systems have become less redistributive in many countries since the mid-1990s. Currently, cash transfers and income taxes reduce income inequality by one quarter among the working-age population. The main reasons for the decline in

redistributive capacity are found on the benefit side: cuts to benefit levels, tightening of eligibility rules to contain expenditures for social protection and the failure of transfers to the lowest income groups to keep pace with earnings growth all contributed.

You just have to love the dry academic language used here, especially in the penultimate point. Contrast this to the following extract from the public relations report[12] on behalf of Income Data Services in the UK:

> "FTSE 100 directors have seen their total earnings increase by an average of 49% in the last financial year, and are now averaging £2,697,664 per annum reveals the latest research by Incomes Data Services (IDS).
>
> IDS say that this increase was even higher than the 43% rise in total earnings for CEOs, which suggests that executive largesse is evenly spread across the board.
>
> Total earnings is fixed pay, salary and benefits, the value of bonuses earned during the year, both cash and deferred, plus the crystallised money value of any long term incentive plan (LTIP) awards and the nominal gains made on the exercise of any share options cashed-in during the year.
>
> FTSE 100 directors saw their average bonus payments increase by 23%, from £737,624 in 2010 to £906,044 in 2011.
>
> Steve Tatton, editor of the IDS report, comments: "Britain's economy may be struggling to return to pre-recession levels of output, but the same cannot be said of FTSE 100 directors' remuneration."
>
> According to the IDS data, the increase in LTIPs and bonus payments received by FTSE 100 directors more than made up for a modest 3.2% growth in base salary that FTSE 100 directors averaged over the last year."

---

[12] Public relations press release issued by Mattison Public Relations on behalf of Incomes Data Services, October 26, 2011

How would you like a bonus equivalent to nearly 4 times the price of the average UK home? I don't know about you, but I think this gives a very clear explanation as to why the wealth gap is growing. You have to wonder why the government finds it necessary to commission a special task force to look at the question of fair pay, don't you? Or how hard the commission would have had to work?

Remember too, all this is at a time when wages for most ordinary workers were frozen and ordinary citizens are finding their standard of living is being squeezed.

Be that as it may, however, it is hardly any wonder that there are signs of a shareholder backlash with shareholders starting to vote against 'excessive' remuneration packages being paid to top executives. It may be just the beginning and a small step, but it is at least curbing executives and their remuneration committees and may help to close the widening gap.

Of course it is hardly surprising that the wealth gap is widening when the income gap is widening. After all, we all know that "it is easier to make money when you have money." In the US, however, it has reached a stage where the top 1% apparently own 35.6% of the national wealth, and even more significantly, 42.4% of the net financial assets that generate financial returns![13] And this is not only the result of a natural phenomenon, but the result of what is described above as "tax and benefit systems that have become less redistributive." To you and me this really means that the wealthy are benefiting from more favourable income tax rates.

You don't even need to look for examples to realise this is the case. You only have to think about the massive industry that exists in the tax field: tax lawyers and tax consultants who specialise in helping high earners (and major corporations) reduce the income tax they pay. Of course it is only the wealthy that can afford these services and who benefit from these tax breaks, even though they are the people who least need it.

---

[13] Economic Policy Institute "State of Working America" 23 March, 2011 Briefing Paper #292.

If you doubt the scale of this you only have to learn what was revealed on a BBC *Panorama* programme[14] about the operations at Barclays Bank. According to this report Barclays had a division called "Structured Capital Markets" which consisted of 100 people specialising in tax structuring and tax avoidance. This division made £1 billion profit in a single year, and all the staff received a bonus of 10% or an average of £1 million each. So just think if Barclays made £1 billion profit how many multiples of that they saved their customers, and at what cost to a struggling public purse, that was having to pick up the costs of the additional benefits payable to people who had lost their jobs or who were due be laid off as a result of the economic downturn caused by – oh yes, the banks.

For evidence of the wealthy benefiting from this you need look no further than well-publicised reports that:

- Jimmy Carr, a top UK comedian, was "one of thousands of wealthy Britons paying as little as one per cent income tax" as a result of using an offshore scheme[15]
- In 2010 Mitt Romney, the Republican candidate for the US presidency in 2012, only paid tax at a rate of 13.9% on net income of $16.5 million[16]
- Warren Buffet, the world's richest man, only paid a tax rate of 11.06% in 2010 on a taxable income of $39,814,784[17]

The list could go on, but I am sure you get the point.

The extent to which vested interests have taken control of the system, mainly through perpetuating the conventional wisdom that the wealthy create more jobs and, therefore, deserve their tax reductions in order to stimulate the economy, is frightening. Now don't get me wrong, I am no socialist apologist and I am the first to recognise that these people do

---

[14] Aired on BBC television on Monday 11th February, 2013.
[15] Report in the Daily Telegraph 19th June 2012
[16] Report in the Washington Post 24th January 2012
[17] Source Forbes Magazine – undated web page.

contribute more to the general economy and that to tax them at punitive rates would be more damaging to the economy and exacerbate the kind of behaviour that I am criticising.

What is particularly frightening, however, is the extent to which, by completely disregarding the lessons of Henry Ford, we have created an economic malfeasance that has endangered not just the economy, but fermented the kind of anger we have seen with the Occupy movements and which could pose a threat to democracy itself if things are not turned around soon.

Yet once again there is nothing new here. More than a century ago Woodrow Wilson warned, "The government, which was designed for the people, has got into the hands of the bosses and their employers, the special interests. An invisible empire has been set up above the forms of democracy." Once again it seems as though conventional wisdom has been allowed to take root and has choked off any misgivings.

SO WHAT CAN WE DO ABOUT IT?

"I am tired of hearing that democracy does not work. Of course it does not work. We are supposed to work it."

ALEXANDER WOOLLCOTT

The short-comings of democracy have been in evidence long before today. In fact, given the misgivings about democracy expressed by people as diverse as Plato and Woodrow Wilson, you really have to wonder if Winston Churchill got it wrong when he said it was "the worst form of government except for all the others" especially when he also said, "The best argument against democracy is a five minute conversation with the average voter." Comments like this bring you back to wondering if democracy isn't actually an impossible ideal, and whether Churchill's ranking it, effectively, by comparison only as "least worst", is not actually an invitation to identify a better form. All this makes it even more remarkable that we take so much for granted and don't do more to safeguard and improve it.

The reason we haven't is because during the boom years we were enjoying the benefits of a higher standard of living and so we weren't too worried if others were getting more than their fair share of the pie. It is only now that we are learning that these living standards were built on false foundations and not only cannot be maintained but are – in a sense – having to be repaid. that we are waking up to the reality. Only now are we becoming aware of the threat to democracy. So, will we take the action necessary to negate it, or will we only start to act when it is too late?

The problem is that when you take something for granted you do not usually see or recognise the threats; and we in the democratic world do generally tend to take democracy for granted. Yet, like any human organisation or institution, democracy is not indestructible, and is subject to constant forces of erosion. The analogy is apt. Erosion takes place continuously, but it is only after time that you become aware of the effects of those destructive forces at work, by which time it is too late.

Democracy faces similar threats. While some of the forces attacking it can be blatant there are many others that are more subtle and, like the forces of erosion, can be invisible – or at least subtle enough that their effects are more difficult to detect. As with erosion these forces constantly, continuously and inexorably wear it down, attacking where the structure is weakest.

We have just seen two areas where democracy is most susceptible to these forces and we will be looking at them again later. There is, however, one more intrinsic weakness, about which we need to be aware and safeguard against – one we have actually touched upon earlier – the "by" element of government.

ELECTED LEADERSHIP

Webster's Unabridged Dictionary defines the verb "lead" in part as "to guide by holding the hand, pulling a rope, etc.; to guide or conduct by showing the way; to direct; to guide the course or direction." Building on that definition, I would therefore say a leader is someone who has the right to guide others as a result of superior experience or expertise or competence. This in turn implies a merited trust as a result of:

- Adherence to sound principles;
- An understanding of the role and the requisite knowledge and ability to respond to the challenges that come with the role;
- An ability to inspire others and create shared values that win the trust and following of the people whom they are leading.

If you accept that definition then the concept of an "elected leader" is actually a syllogism that, upon deeper examination, does nothing more than create a virtual oxymoron. This is because a "leader" who has to act in accordance with his people's wishes, rather than in the manner demanded by the situation, is actually a puppet and not a leader. Isn't this the situation in most democracies?

The problem is that elected leaders have to act in accordance with their electorate's wishes or face losing office. While it is appropriate that they have to be held accountable for their actions the office often becomes more important than the reason they ran for it in the first place. Consequently they remain a prisoner of their electoral platform or "election manifesto" and are not able to respond to current affairs in the best way possible. If you don't believe that, just think about the media outcry when an "elected leader" fails to honour an election pledge or tries to introduce a "policy U-turn." Thus it really becomes a case of the tail wagging the dog: the leaders actions are dictated by the people they are leading and it is almost impossible to move away from mass-opinion. How can you expect leaders to be true leaders in such situations or to ever come up with new ideas that challenge the conventional wisdom in such circumstances? So you end up with "follow leadership" rather than the intelligent, innovative and inspiring leadership of the sort that democracy demands. Of course that is why you end up with government that is not really *for* the people, with the kind of awful results we have just been considering.

That may perhaps be why Winston Churchill described democracy as the "least worst" form of government. But what kind of future do you think democracy has if we continue with leaders who are incapable of being innovative and, in repeated scenarios, only respond to what they think the people want? There will definitely come a time when people will want to revisit some of those "other forms." In these tough economic times this is possibly more likely than ever. It would be better for all of us if these changes were evolutionary, but – as the Occupy movement hints – people are disgruntled and thus there is the very real danger that they are more likely to follow historical precedent and be revolutionary. Unless we act now.

THE EROSION OF EQUALITY

CHAPTER THREE
AWFUL ACCOUNTING

> **"There are three types of accountant – those that can count and those that can't."**
>
> **ANONYMOUS**

Accounting is a profession that has always been the butt of jokes, and as an accountant myself I became used to them a long time ago. I even became inured to the one about the accountant being "the person who comes onto the battlefield after the battle and shoots the wounded." However, I really enjoyed the one above. Not because I know any accountants that cannot count (although as I get more removed from daily number-crunching, I am afraid I might be heading in that direction) but because I believe it is a widely unacknowledged fact that there *are* actually three types of accountant.

Now this isn't something for which the profession can take any credit (or should that be debit?) That is because it is not something accountants set about creating, but is simply the consequence of the fact that there have historically been three generic types of organisation, most commonly identified as:

- Private sector – "For-profit" companies where the business sets out to create a return on the investment for those that "own" the organisation;
- Public sector – "Not-for-profit" Government and NGO organisations;
- Social sector – Charities, community or social enterprise companies, where the ultimate delivery is often provided by volunteers or at a non-commercial rate.

This categorisation has resulted in each developing its own accounting practices and thus ending up with its own accounting principles, conventions and processes. As a result you could quite reasonably say that there are three types of accountant.

While this appears entirely logical and seems reasonable one very unfortunate consequence is that it has resulted in each becoming a specialist area – not just in terms of accounting but generally across the board. This has made it very difficult for people to move from a career in one area to a career in another. In turn this has made them more insular and isolated and boundaries have been created, which make it more difficult for new ideas to travel between them.

This has been particularly noticeable in the division between private and public sector, where each has developed a strong disdain for the other. Of course this has its roots in the different objectives of the two. The bottom-line focus of the private sector fuels the continuous objective of more efficient and effective use of resources, which is anathema to the service focus of the public sector. In contrast, the community focus of the public sector, which makes service paramount and the use of resources almost incidental, is anathema to the private sector. Thus the public sector considers the private sector to be brutal, cold-hearted and unsympathetic, while the private sector views the public sector as administratively maladroit with expenditure that is ill-conceived, unnecessary or excessive.

All this has been exacerbated by the economic crisis. The private sector, concerned by the growth in government and the mounting costs associated with it, is demanding greater prudence and austerity in public affairs. On the other hand the public sector, already feeling the pain of these efforts and fearing the effects on its service capability, is resisting these efforts which it considers to be bringing private sector standards and values to the public sector.

But all this conflict stems from the categorisation of the different organisations which, yet again, is nothing else but convention or unchallenged conventional wisdom.

The categorisation is rooted in the different goals and values of the organisations. Yet if you work from a higher principle, each type of organisation should be looking to deliver its products or services at the lowest possible cost, simply because not to do so is to be wasteful and to abuse resources. In other words they should all be looking to offer best value, and thus should all have the same values. In fact, morally, both the public sector and the social sector have a greater responsibility to minimise their costs than the private sector. Why? Because they are spending other people's money!

So the accounting profession should definitely not take any credit for the fact there are three types of accountant. On the contrary, it should be blamed for dereliction of duty. How could the profession allow a system to develop where the public sector is "managed by budget" and government departments rush out to spend all their expenditure budgets in order not to have a reduced budget the next year? Surely the wag was right who said, "An accountant is someone who knows the cost of everything and the value of nothing."

If you doubt it, let's take a fresh look at a topical subject – sustainability. Concerns about the environment have brought sustainability to the front of many people's minds. Championed initially by a fringe few who were prepared to challenge the conventional wisdom and who were regarded as kooks by the rest of us, they have created the "green" movement that is now pervading all aspects of life; including the bottom-lined private sector who have realised that their businesses will not survive if they are not more socially responsible and do not do more to safeguard our fragile planet and protect its valuable resources. Isn't that also a reflection on accountants for not recognising the true value of resources used in production?

As I pointed out in *A Feeling of Worth*, Newton's Third Law of Motion teaches us that "for every action there is an equal and opposite reaction." This means that, scientifically, there can be no such thing as profit. Yet we continue to use profit as the primary driver for the large part of our commercial and economic activity. If accountants are to make a more useful contribution they are going to have to start focusing less on the traditional accounting conventions and pay more attention to value.

> **"If you look at the history of the American capital market there is probably no innovation more important than the idea of generally accepted accounting principles."**
>
> **LAWRENCE SANDERS**

In the light of what we have just seen this could be a very frightening statement. Of course we accountants need principles to govern our behaviour and to some extent to help ensure that others follow them, too. However, we saw earlier how the income and wealth gaps are widening and some of the reasons why, including a basic failure to follow generally accepted economic principles. It would therefore seem that we accountants are falling well short of the standards the world needs us to follow. As my old school reports used to say, "Could do better" – a lot better! So let's see what else we can do to broaden our horizons and make our contribution more meaningful, more useful and more valuable.

CHAPTER FOUR
PERMITTED PLUNDER & LEGALISED LARCENY

> "Every corporation exists for the public good – to be useful and beneficial to society. Without this awareness it is impossible to mobilize a workforce to maximum advantage."
>
> **KONOSUKE MATSUSHITA**

This statement encapsulates the fundamental principle that sustains any organisation. As long as it meets that criterion it is likely to survive and thrive. Unfortunately, there is a plethora of examples that suggest this principle is being lost to sight and, as a consequence, our whole economic system is at risk and our whole environment is under very real threat. In such circumstances it is pretty easy to come up with examples.

What these examples really show, however, is how the power has shifted and the concepts of democracy that we have been looking at as our basic ideal have been pirated, pillaged and plundered. They illustrate not just the destructive elements at play, but also how these are being allowed to go unchallenged as a result of conventional wisdom that is based on false or incorrect premises.

So let's press on without any further ado.

BUSINESS AS BOSS

It has become very fashionable to blame the banks for the 2008 economic crisis, and the subsequent Great Recession that we have been looking at elsewhere. Certainly there is no doubt that the ridiculous, risky and unchecked lending played a massive part in this. The banks, however, are not alone in their culpability, but have been actively and passively assisted in their efforts by government.

Think for a moment about the growth in government that I wrote about earlier. Government is a non-productive player in the economy. Its primary source of revenue is taxes and thus it relies on tax-payers to finance or fund its expenditure. The bigger government grows, the more it spends; the more it spends the more revenue it needs to acquire and thus more taxes. It becomes a vicious circle.

What, however, is one of the government's main sources of tax revenue? Corporate taxes! Consequently, in order to safeguard this revenue source, government has a vested interest in profitable business. As a result, government policy is increasingly driven by the interests of business. Conventional wisdom tells us that business doing well means the economy is doing well and that is good for everyone. Of course that is true, and it would be foolish in the extreme to suggest otherwise, but where does democracy fit in all this? It doesn't. Government is no longer for the people, but for business. Thus "big business" is the *de facto* boss in controlling economic and political affairs. You cannot get into government or stay in government without pandering to the interests of big business, and of all businesses, banks and financial institutions are amongst the most powerful.

KING OF THE 'HOOD

Financial institutions are in a uniquely powerful position *vis-à-vis* other businesses, because the only way that governments can continue to operate in the short term when tax revenues are insufficient is by borrowing. And who do they borrow from? That's right – the financial institutions and banks; directly or indirectly. Thus over time these organisations have become extremely powerful because:

- With the scale of national debt, government is too beholden to them;

- They have control over so many other finances that the domino effect is too great.

Not only is that why it has been said that banks are too big to fail and governments have rushed in to rescue them, rather than take the easier option of simply bailing out the depositors; it is also why, despite all the vociferous indignation, there have been no real consequences for their failures. (A cynic might also add that this is also because bank executives are the biggest supporters and financial contributors to election campaigns!)

MODERN BANK ROBBERY

The days of Jesse James and his ilk robbing banks are long gone. Today it is the other way round and it is the banks doing the robbing – and on a grander scale than ever before. And who are they robbing? Well for starters it is the government, and there are several very good reasons for starting there.

- Government is neither a real person nor a single person and is therefore less likely to realise when it is being robbed. Put another way, government simply isn't smart enough!
- Government has so much money flowing through its coffers that it is unlikely to notice when it is being robbed. It is rather like the extremely wealthy person who is so rich that they do not notice when their advisor/banker/secretary/servant is embezzling money in relatively small amounts.
- As we have just seen, government is dependent on business and especially on banks, so it cannot risk protesting. Even if it were to do so it would risk being exposed as complicit, incapable, incompetent, or all three.
- When action is considered, the banks blackmail government by threatening to relocate their corporate headquarters to another country, and thereby destroy jobs and the revenue base – such as it is – that government relies on.

Of course this is all possible because the conventional wisdom has it that this is how things work.

We have already seen some evidence of how this works in Chapter Two albeit at the individual level, when we looked at the examples of Jimmy Carr, Mitt Romney and Warren Buffet. Here, we are looking at it on a corporate basis. So now let's see how they do it.

1. The banks begin by setting up various tax avoidance schemes to reduce their corporate tax liabilities.
2. If necessary, they convince government that the revenues paid in bonuses to executives as a result of increased profits will compensate for some of the revenue foregone (forgetting to mention that similar private schemes also exist.)
3. Then, not content with just benefiting from their lower tax payments, they start selling these schemes to their clients and other tax advisors to market on their behalf, thus increasing their own profits.
4. Finally, when government's tax revenues fall (and government accepts that it is merely because of declining profits and/or the depressed economy) they lend them the money they need to make up their shortfall – at a profit.

The scale of this kind of operation was laid bare in that Panorama programme on BBC television[18] I mentioned previously, which revealed that Barclays Bank alone had set up a "Structured Capital Markets" division of 100 people whose sole purpose was tax structuring and tax avoidance. In 2010 this division alone made a profit of £1 billion. Now you cannot imagine that Barclays itself would have paid taxes at anything like the normal corporate rate for such a scheme, if in fact they paid any at all. Likewise you can only imagine that to make a profit of that scale that the tax savings for the customers would have been several multiples more. So the revenue foregone by the government must have been in the tens

---

[18] Aired on BBC television on Monday 11th February, 2013.

of billions, and this was just *one* bank. Multiply that across the entire banking tax avoidance sector and the scale of the revenue lost must be astronomic.

Certainly this does not fit with Konosuke Matsushita's words at the start of this chapter. And once again what is particularly frightening here is what appears to be the lack of economic understanding behind this behaviour. In a time of economic crisis when the government is trying to encourage growth while playing down the national debt and struggling with unemployment because of all the jobs lost as a result of this recession, it is not just anti-social, but also extremely undemocratic, and, it could be argued, bordering on the criminal. Yet even worse than the short-term damage this behaviour causes, is the fact that it is not only unsustainable in the longer-term, but it also critically damaging to the future national economy.

Yet there has hardly been any outcry in response to the programme which was released shortly after the new CEO of Barclays announced a new set of standards aimed at rebuilding the bank's reputation. Nowhere is there any hint or mention of any kind of reparation and neither has the government said anything. And remember this government is supposed to be "by" you and "for" you! (Even then that ignores the fact that government is "of" you and that you are, therefore, actually the victim!)

MOMMY, I'M SCARED

If that is not frightening enough there is more. This example is only one bank out of many, and the whole banking industry is already being shown up in a bad light. The scenario I have just depicted is a robbery of government through industrial scale tax avoidance schemes. But the government is not the only direct target of modern bank robberies. We have also been targeted at the individual level as evidenced by:

- The Libor scandal and a large number of banks that have been investigated and fined for manipulating the

lending rates at who knows what additional cost to you and me.
- The gigantic mis-selling of payment protect insurance (PPI) which has resulted in banks having to pay large fines as well as repaying billions for policies incorrectly (fraudulently) sold.

It is all very well with Barclays coming out with a new set of standards and declaring that the five values of respect, integrity, service, excellence and stewardship will be at the heart of all their dealings from now on, but those were the core values that I would have expected from any bank all along – including the time when these robberies were being perpetrated. I still have no idea how these values came to be so readily buried or what the cost of these shenanigans might have been to me and I still worry about what else they might have been doing to rip me off. It is also a concern that no other bank has made any similar commitment, and I wonder, therefore, if the competitive banking environment prevents such a commitment and thus how long it may last even at Barclays, let alone if it is simply wishful thinking when it comes to the rest of the industry.[19]

You also have to question the effectiveness of the fines levied, particularly at a time when the banks that were bailed out after the financial crisis are still owned by the tax-payer, which means that we are the ones paying anyway. Not only that, it is also us who cough-up to fund the banks' new capital requirements as well as their other initiatives to make good their past losses. (I cannot be the only one to have been

---

[19] It would seem that my misgivings were justified. The new CEO introducing these policies has already been fired. Reports indicate that this is because he lost the confidence of his Board, who felt he was taking the task of reducing investment banking activities too seriously, significantly affecting profitability. This begs the question as to whether the bank was ever really committed to the new policies he introduced and they were merely window dressing or whether competitive forces make backsliding inevitable. Either way it doesn't say much for the corrective measures taken to prevent recurrences of the excesses of the industry. Still, the £28 million termination package reported in the Sunday Times on 12 July 2015, won't hurt him too much and will prevent him from saying or doing anything that could jeopardise any return to the old ways.

irked by a letter from my bank telling me that they were reducing their interest rates on deposits because of the record low prime rate while – in the same letter – announcing that they were *increasing* their lending rates! Just how stupid do they think their ~~victims~~ customers are?!)

But there is more to it even than that. The whole system that I have described still gives me conniptions because I don't see any real signs that it is being constructively tackled. Let me explain more about why I say that.

BACK TO BARCLAYS

Let's return for a moment to that Panorama programme about Barclays. It revealed that in 2010-11 the bank paid £1.4 billion in dividends and £6 billion in bonuses. This means that the staff received more than 4 times the amount that the shareholders got. As you will see later, I am all in favour of employees receiving a more representative share of profits, but I still wasn't aware that Barclays had become that socialistic. Furthermore, £6 billion in bonuses in just one year seems incredibly excessive when the total increase in profit before tax over the preceding 10 years was less than £2.4 billion. That certainly seems excessive to me, particularly when the presenter also announced that, according to the best analysis that experts could produce from the accounts, the then CEO had been paid more than £120 million over 6 years.

The questionable morality behind these earnings aside, this not only reinforces my points about the disparate earnings and the widening earnings gap that I mentioned in Chapter Two, but it also underscores my concerns about the whole system. The likelihood that anyone actually paid the full going rate of income tax that you and I would pay is so remote that I doubt any self-respecting bookie would even take a bet.

SOMETHING ROTTEN IN THE STATE

It seems unfair to keep picking on Barclays, especially when it is only an example of one among many and may not perhaps even be the worst offender. Who knows?

One thing, however, is very clear: moral standards generally are not as high as we would like them to be. The horsemeat in beef products throughout Europe shows that this is not just a British "disease." It is also indicative of how far we have to go if we are to restore any faith in the system and in democracy itself. This, however, brings me back to my earlier point about the need to make democracy more relevant and more "bottom-up." There has to be a greater moral conscience across the board at all levels along with the peer pressure that will ensure people act as soon as they encounter anything that is out of order. At present we are moving further away from that prospect – and true democracy – rather than closer to it. This is unacceptable in a world that is more crowded and more inter-dependent than ever before and, therefore, one that needs to utilise its resources more efficiently and effectively.

Unfortunately, because of its ties to business and its own sense of self-importance, there seems to be no leadership in government or in political circles to take up the challenge. The two sectors seem to be complicit in maintaining the *status quo*, perhaps partly because they are so steeped in the traditional way of viewing things that they are incapable of moving beyond convention. We will move on now to explore one of those other conventions – the political system.

CHAPTER FIVE
POLICY PERVERSION

> "The trite saying that honesty is the best policy has met with just criticism. The real honest man is honest from conviction of what is right, not from policy."
>
> **ROBERT E LEE**

From what we have just seen it would appear that the belief that honesty is a policy has permeated through society. As a result it is not seen as a standard, but rather as an expediency; to be adopted or not as the circumstances dictate and dependent on the chances of being found out or not. In fact it would appear from the example of the banks that even the chances of being found out do not ensure it. Being found out is a small price to pay if there are no personal consequences.

Such expediency reminds me of that apocryphal story of the alleged conversation between HG Wells and Isadora Duncan.

HG Wells: "Will you sleep with me for a million pounds?"

Isadora Duncan: "Yes."

HG Wells: "Will you sleep with me for five pounds?"

Isadora Duncan, irately: "What kind of lady do you take me for?"

HG Wells: "We've already established that. We are now simply haggling over the price."

And that is the problem with policies generally. They are the poor counterfeit of, and no real substitute for, principle; rooted in shallow soil and easily overcome by circumstance. On the other hand, principle has the tenancy of truth and is permanent.

Unfortunately, in the modern age, policy appears to reign supreme. This is why we are a long way removed from Margaret Thatcher's belief that "Politics is philosophy in action."

You need to look no further than politics to see this (although perhaps this should not be surprising, given the root meaning of the word politics!) Before every election parties get together and prepare manifestos of policies which then become the bible for their campaign and the benchmark by which they are judged when elected. Thus any shift of policy is seen as an act of treachery, and policy tends to become a handcuff rather than a help.

Imagine that you were going into battle and you had a general who was prepared to change his tactics if the situation "on the ground" demanded it and another who would stick to the same tactics no matter what. Under which one would you rather serve? Of course it would be the adaptable one – the other would be an "at all costs" kind of guy, where those costs could be excessive and would be more likely than otherwise to include you.

Yet when it comes to political leaders we tend to prefer the latter type. We admire their "dogged determination" and completely fail to recognise that – as we have seen – they too are leading a fight and need to be tactically aware and, therefore, flexible. If this image seems inapt, don't forget it is politicians who start the wars and the generals who end up fighting them!

The promotion of policy over principle, however, has greater ramifications. It leads to a proliferation of policies and tactics, and that in turn means there is more to fight over. Every different policy or tactic creates its own opponents. This is perhaps a primary reason for politics becoming more strident and aggressive over the years, particularly when people feel emotionally tied to specific policies and cannot afford to be more flexible. This is compounded by policies being layered on top of existing policies and thereby diluting, distorting or even destroying the effectiveness of the original policy and becoming further and further removed from the principles from which they were initially developed. This is exacerbated by the constant yo-yoing between different parties when each has the opportunity to govern.

You have to ask yourself how much political conflict could have been, and could still be, avoided if debate started from principle rather than policy; and, as a result, what savings there could be of both time and money, let alone the ancillary costs when the differences degenerate.

To illustrate what I am driving at let us take a look at the party political system.

POOPING THE PARTIES

Political parties are our means to categorise, congregate and conjoin like-minded thinkers. As such they seem a perfectly logical means to funnel the population and create a workable system to elect and govern: to determine the "by" people who run our democracies "for" us. At the end of the day, however, they are basically just part of a system and no system is likely to be perfect. Most systems will have flaws; the more complex the issue the more difficult it is to design a system and the more flaws it is likely to have. Thus any system requires periodic reviews to assess how well it is working, what flaws there are and how they need to be addressed in order to be "fit for purpose." The more complex the system, the more important such reviews become and, as we have already seen, determining the "by" element of democracy is its biggest challenge. This means that this system should be reviewed regularly. Unfortunately, this is never done.

Our political systems are left to run in much the same way as they always have, with possibly the only "tuning" that is ever done being the re-alignment of the electoral boundaries and the updating of the voter rolls – as the governing party tries to gain some voting advantage. So once again we are left to convention and once again deeper consideration shows unfortunate results. There is a definite case for arguing that current political systems are not working and that the solution has now actually become part of the problem.

Given the existence of an already established party, the first step for that party when preparing for an election is the creation of its manifesto. Here some group – hopefully the most intelligent with the highest integrity and clearest vision, but perhaps the most hard-working, the most dedicated or the most passionate or some other unique trait, but often possibly those who can simply better spare the time – get together and build on the constitution of the party, and (ostensibly) the principles it espouses, to create policies, in theory with an eye to how the population at large will benefit. These are then collated and presented to all party members at the party congress or party conference.

This Party "party" lasts several days, with mainly members and the press attending. There is a lot of networking and social activity as people jostle to voice their opinions and become better known and more popular, all around a plethora of speeches as various leading lights in the party present key aspects of the manifesto, which the members then vote to either accept or reject. The approved policies are then incorporated into an election manifesto and elected representatives (along with would-be elected representatives) proceed to canvas the general public to win their support and secure the votes to win a seat in a legislative "house", where they will endeavour to turn these policies into law, by virtue of a common majority.

This may be the "least worst" scenario that Churchill depicted, but there are a number of inherent flaws in this system.

- The policies are drawn up by like-minded people, coming at an issue from a particular perspective or point of view. This means that there is already a bias to the perceived problems, causes and solutions.
- People are naturally more concerned about some issues than others. Consequently they do not necessarily give the same level of attention to those in which they are less interested.
- Once policy is agreed, party members are generally obliged to commit to them. This means that they have

to "take the whip" and follow the party line when the issue comes up in parliament.
- With each party having to adhere to its agreed policy on any specific issue, debate can become more acrimonious and the opportunity for the evolution of a modified solution that incorporates different elements of each becomes less likely.
- Acrimonious dispute of this ilk is enabled by the lack of objective clarity in the issues and policies being debated, leading to confrontational politics that damages the credibility of the system and the people populating it - combined with the inevitable points scoring that goes with the party system.

PARTY TENSIONS

The fact that each party has to accommodate a number of different people with varying shades of opinion on different subjects can also cause extreme tensions within the party and be counterproductive to the party's own overall objectives.

A good example of this is the "Tea Party" faction within the US Republican party. These people, symbolised by Sarah Palin, represented an extreme element within the party, who managed through the vehemence of their policies and the aggressive manner in which they published and promoted them, to shift the overall direction of the party, antagonise the wider population and make the party virtually unelectable when it came time for the elections.

There are similar tensions in the two main parties in the UK. The Conservatives struggle to keep their more extreme, "right-wing" and anti-European Union members from splintering the party, while the Labour party struggles with the out-and-out socialist elements and the power of the Trade Unions who provide a considerable part of the party finances.

All this means that the policies which result are a compromise that may not be something with which the wider population actually feels comfortable and which may not be the best option for the country as a whole.

POLICY-LOCK

Rigid adherence to defined policy and the inability to be more flexible and look for consensus or compromise can also lead to something that you could call "policy-lock." The impasse over the national deficit in the US is an extreme example of this kind of "policy-lock".

In August 2011 the US was brought to the very edge of a crisis that would make it ungovernable. It could not legally exceed its debt limit but the bills that were due meant that such an increase would be inevitable. However, the Republican majority would not approve this without a plan to reduce the deficit and they demanded future spending cuts to achieve this. On the other hand the Democrats argued that any future deficit reduction plan had to include tax increases. As a result the issue went to the wire before a compromise bill was signed.

At that time President Barack Obama said, "Is this the deal I would have preferred? No. But this compromise does make a serious down payment on the deficit reduction we need, and gives each party a strong incentive to get a balanced plan done before the end of the year."

He appeared to be right for there was a huge incentive for both sides to get a better deal. The law said that if the two parties couldn't come up with a better solution, two things would happen:

1. The borrowing limit would automatically increase by another $1.2 trillion.
2. Automatic, across-the-board spending cuts called a "sequester" would kick in

Conservatives did not want to raise the debt ceiling any more, and liberals did not want social programs slashed, so it seemed like the strong-handed tactic might actually work.

Yet despite this the lawmakers failed to act and in March 2013 "sequestration" kicked in.

Here is a paraphrased explanation of sequestration[20] that I downloaded from the internet.[21]

> **Sequestration Is a Silly Way to Do Business**
>
> Imagine you had a small business that employed ten people. Two were brilliant workers who added tremendous value to your company and increased its profitability. Two of your employees were slackers who seriously underperformed in their duties. The rest were average workers.
>
> Now let's say the bad economy was affecting your business and forced you to make a 20% cut in your payroll. Which of these two scenarios would be smarter?
>
> 1. Fire the two underperforming employees, eliminating 20% of your workforce; or
>
> 2. Slash 20% of all 10 employees' salary on an equal basis.
>
> A wise business owner would never pick #2 and punish his star employees in order to be "fair" to the slackers. That's plain silly.
>
> But that's what a government sequester is all about: Every department pays equally. Across-the board cuts without taking into consideration the value of the program.

Now it turned out that this is not actually the case and that there were a large number of exclusions to the sequestration process. In fact the hardest hit area will be Defence and it's just possible that this solution may have given the Republi-

---

[20] "Sequestration" as referred to here is simply a US term to describe the forced budget cutting as a result of the fact that the US has reached its constitutional borrowing limit and the impasse in negotiations between the parties. It does not have the normal meaning of the legal seizure of property and has no other direct relevance to the subject. As far as I know "sequestration" does not apply anywhere other than the US, which is the only country to have a constitutional borrowing constraint – although this was something I argued for in 'A Feeling of Worth'.

[21] Source http://theelevationgroup.com/sequestration-outrage-obamas-salary-untouched

cans a "get-out-of-jail-free" card, enabling them to support a move, for which they dare not actually vote in favour. If so, no wonder my parents always told me, "Politics is a dirty business." Maybe Albert Camus expressed it more diplomatically when he said, "By definition a government has no conscience. Sometimes it has a policy but nothing more." Either way, we are back to the changeability of policy, which can also be called "expediency."

There may be some people who would argue that this shows just how flexible democracy can be and why it is thus such a good system. For my part, however, I find it too Machiavellian and a very poor indictment on the party system and the inherent dangers it poses. If you ever look at some of the blog comments on the internet and read some of the intolerant vitriol that I have seen, you would also quake and ask yourself if the system can actually survive. This is all down to the party system and what I can only call policy perversion and, as I hope to demonstrate, is all unnecessary and avoidable.

OTHER DRAWBACKS OF PARTY POLITICS

All this is before you even get into the system of electing people and ensuring that they remain accountable for their actions!

This is an area that is more open to scrutiny with the validity of elections results being questioned everywhere from the US to Zimbabwe. (Who knows how different history might have been if Al Gore had won the Florida recount and become US president instead of George Bush!) However, it is not possible vote rigging or voter intimidation or tampering with counts that concerns us here. Rather it is simply whether voting on a party basis is actually the best option to begin with (and to answer your unasked question; No, I don't understand the concept of voting in a one-party state either!)

We have just looked at how the party system can lead to "policy perversion" but you need to remember too that this is in what I have described as an "upside-down democracy." This begs the question, "How meaningful is it to vote for a candidate you don't know, from a list of candidates that you don't know, based on a number of policies which might or might not be relevant to you or your voting constituency?"

That may sound cynical and it is your duty to meet and listen to the different candidates and hear what they think before you actually vote. This is part of good citizenship and the role that you are required to play to be one of the people "by" whom you are governed, for in electing a candidate you are, after all, simply choosing a representative to act on your behalf in the way you would expect.

But as they will all be likely to put on their best appearances and avoid any controversy during their campaign, how well can you really get to know them or gauge how well they will look after your interests? How do you gauge their competency or their ability to be creative and come up with new, different and better ways of doing things when they are confronted with a new challenge or when traditional solutions no longer work? How do you know whether they will be "expedient" or not? Remember that their continuing in that role depends on their ability to satisfy the majority of their constituents, and so may not depend on such innovative capabilities but rather the exact opposite – their ability to conform. Ralph Nader was right when he said, "Once you don't vote with your ideals ... that has serious undermining effects. It erodes the moral basis of our democracy."

So in the light of this, you can see how difficult it is for you to really tell who is the right person to represent you and look after your interests. Thus it is hardly surprising that you will be more likely to simply cast your eye over the list and then vote for the candidate who represents the political party, for which you usually vote. It would be very interesting to research how many people always vote for candidates from the same party. I expect the percentage is quite high, which means that any change in government is due to a very small minority and/or an increasing number of voters who have despaired of the party system and elected not to vote at all.

MUGWUMPS UNITE

What is a competent government? How would you define one and, more importantly, how can you ensure you get one? I don't know about you but I worry about the cyclical nature of government with the constant swing from one party being in government to the next. This inevitably means that the minute you get a new government in power, you have (at least some) inexperienced people in control. Never mind the fact that every time it happens they proceed to undo the policies of the previous government and implement their own. To my way of thinking, although that ought to prevent people "doing a Mugabe" and continuing in office long after they have passed their sell-by date and no-one really wants them, that cannot be in the best long-term interests of the country.

Once again it would seem that we have come up with a systemic solution that has become a convention that is seldom, if ever, properly evaluated. How does being a leader of a political party equip one to become the leader of a democratic country and to run it?

Whether you agree with this or not, in the light of all this you have to question the blind acceptance of our party-based voting system and the lack of scrutiny to which it is subjected. A two-party system such as those you find in the UK and USA can bring you the kind of deadlock you are currently seeing in the US, while a multi-party democracy can create the kind of instability that has bedevilled Italy. The problem is that both become a laughing stock. To rely on systems that may be so fundamentally flawed and on which the ultimate survival of the planet may depend is foolhardy in the extreme. At the very least you want to know that the people by whom you are being governed are the best people for the role. And it is highly doubtful that the party political system – which we take so for granted – gives you that.

CHAPTER SIX
ERRANT EDUCATION

> "Democracy demands an educated and informed electorate."
>
> **THOMAS JEFFERSON**

No matter how you elect the people by whom you wish to be governed, you need to:

a) Choose the best people for the job; and
b) Assess whether they are doing a good job or not and replace them if they are not.

Both capabilities demand that the people doing the judging are competent to do so – a point that makes Jefferson's words a statement of the obvious.

It's a cliché that, "In a democracy you get the government you deserve." While that may be literally true as the unavoidable consequence of majority rule, it is an unfair and unfortunate downside of democracy for the people who voted differently. It may be even worse than that, for in a world that is increasingly integrated and inter-connected, those decisions can have increasingly widespread consequences. This makes it even more imperative that you have a process that ensures the best possible results.

Unfortunately the indications are that we are a long way removed from that. Nor will we ever get there if we continue to rely on systems that depend on populist opinion. You need look no further than the situation in Europe to see where I am coming from on this one. A number of European countries if not already bankrupt like Greece, are on the verge of bankruptcy – Italy, Portugal, Spain, France and the UK to name a few. Yet, what happens when the governments are forced to take action to reduce spending and introduce "austerity measures"? The people strike, the extremists riot, the government is thrown out and a more popular government elected on a platform of refusing to bow down to the economic pressures.

There are in fact two distinct issues here.

- The dichotomy with elected leadership and the difficulty, verging on the impossibility, of electing people capable of "leading" the people rather than pandering to the popular vote.
- The inadequacy of the existing system and the incompetence of past and current leaders who have allowed this situation to develop in the first place.

The first issue is covered elsewhere and there is no need to belabour the point here. The second is a very real problem and one to which we need to wake up and address pretty promptly.

TURNING THE SHIP AROUND

The riots experienced in the UK and different countries in Europe are a serious warning sign that we are sitting on a powder keg. The near record levels of unemployment, the declining standard of living that many are experiencing and the widening wealth gap that I have outlined, are all evidence of a failing system. If nothing is done to turn the situation around, there is a great danger that democracies in the western world will actually become anarchic and ungovernable.

The big question is, "Where do you begin to turn things around?"

For me the starting point has to be the education system. It is very common, almost fashionable, to bemoan falling educational standards, but this is not really what I am getting at here. What I am talking about goes far deeper than curricula and grades, and actually goes to the very purpose of education.

Conventional wisdom has it that the point of education is to create a population of emerging workers capable of performing to the level of the demands made on them by a rapidly changing workplace. However, education is about so much more than creating a pool of subject matter experts to meet the demands of an increasingly sophisticated workplace. The problem with that perspective is that it sets the goal at the barest minimum. Factor in the good intentions of well-meaning people who demand an equal delivery of education and you have a double whammy that persistently has the effect of lowering universal standards.

Here you might want to accuse me of arguing against myself and the democratic principle of equality that I have been espousing. However, that is not the case. It is a matter of common arithmetic as well as basic economics that it is easier to bring the standard of the elite down than to raise the masses up to the elite standard. Thus the crux of the issue here is not so much one of equality but one of equitability.

CREATING GOOD CITIZENS

You don't have to be a teacher to understand that students have different capabilities as well as different maturity levels and maturity rates. Nature and nurture may each play a part here but it should be the role of education to identify and ensure that those with ability are encouraged to optimise their capabilities in order to fulfil their potential. Not to do so is a waste. On the other hand, teaching people to a standard beyond their capability is just as much of a waste. Thus you could argue that trying to provide equal education creates waste at both ends. That is why trying to provide equal education is fallacious and a fool's errand. Teaching students to the level of their current capabilities may not be equal in semantic terms but it is certainly equitable, and as long as every student is being taught to their capability you could argue that it *is* equal – it is certainly good enough.

However, that is only part of the issue and may even be a diversion. The key point is that the purpose of education is – or should be – to create better citizens.

That of course is a much wider purpose, but it is one that, unfortunately, is either not recognised or has lip service paid to it and is not properly understood. The exaggerated emphasis on creating "commercial cannon-fodder" (people capable of going into the workplace and being productive) has been based on the convention that a good career is the route to prosperity and a good life and is therefore automatically good for everyone. This has enabled the effective subordination of the good citizen bit to such an extent that sight of it has been almost totally lost.

Being law-abiding, prepared for (and capable) of joining the productive workforce, and a good citizen *is not* one and the same thing. Citizenship is an acknowledgement of being part of a community and thus necessitates a community focus, along with a clear understanding of the obligations and rights of that go with it. This is even more true in a democracy but, unfortunately, is not something that is covered in sufficient depth in our education systems.

Not only does being a good citizen in a democracy require a good understanding of all the issues, at which we have been looking, but it also requires a degree of independence and self-sufficiency that is not appearing to be properly inculcated. Perhaps the fact that current unemployment levels are highest amongst the young people is indicative of this. (I am not saying this is the case, but simply that we should be exploring the possibility more.)

Something that raised this possibility in my mind was the news about the increase in unpaid rent by people receiving benefit payments in the UK, following a change in the way those benefits were paid. Previously rents were paid directly to the landlord but, in an attempt to give these people more dignity and more control over their own lives, the government decided they should be responsible for administering their own affairs. In the areas where this was trialled, rent arrears increased by as much as 50% in just a few months. Whichever way you look at this, it is indicative of poor education; assuming that these people were able to get on with their lives properly before, when their rent was paid, it suggests either:

- That the recipients are incapable of looking after their own affairs; or
- They are absolutely indifferent to their responsibilities.

These are hard times, I know and people in the lower income groups are finding it increasingly difficult to get by. I understand that, but food and shelter form the very base of Maslow's hierarchy of needs,[22] and what person with a modicum of understanding, education and self-respect would not put paying their rent at the top of their priority list? The fact that so many appear incapable of this is surely indicative of an education system that failed to teach the very fundamentals.

Ultimately, despite a higher intelligence than most other creatures, man cannot survive on his own. Anthropologically it is only through working together as part of a larger group that humankind has been able to dominate their environment to the extent it has. However, the scale of this evolution and the sophistication of the technological advances that have accompanied it, have increased the complexity of this interaction. So much so that we have moved beyond the "global village" that Marshall McLuhan[23] described. Now the degree of integration and inter-connectedness means that no nation is independent and that almost everything we do has an impact on the wider world. In such a world, it is imperative that we understand this and act accordingly.

No matter how representative they are, or what proportion of society they represent, the fact that people are unable to manage their own finances is disturbing. However, what makes it really frightening is that these people have an equal vote! In other words, people who cannot manage their own affairs, have the right to choose the "by people" who govern

---

[22] *Maslow's hierarchy of needs* is a theory in psychology proposed by Abraham Maslow in his 1943 paper "A Theory of Human Motivation"
[23] Herbert Marshall McLuhan was a Canadian philosopher of communication theory known for coining the expressions *the medium is the message* and the *global village*, first mentioned in his 1968 book, "War and Peace in the Global Village." He also predicted the World Wide Web almost thirty years before it was invented.

us. How can they decide what is the best for the community and the country, when they cannot even decide what is best for themselves?

Now I am not saying that they should not have the vote, but for heaven's sake let's ensure that we have an education system that prevents, or at least dramatically reduces, this kind of scenario from happening. Thomas Jefferson was 100% correct and this makes it imperative that we have a better educated population. How can we judge – other than from our own self-interest – whether the "by people" are doing a good job "for the people" if we do not understand what good government is?

This requires a more sophisticated education system that covers such core issues as:

- How to manage money and a household
- How government works – where it gets its money from and how it spends it
- Why voting is important
- How to judge whether government is doing a good job
- How to change things when you don't think government is doing a good job
- Etc.

Of course you may challenge this and ask how many of us really understand all this. However, that is precisely the point. While it is relatively easy to pick on a particular segment of society and point fingers at them, good government depends on our ability to elect a good government. As ever the proof of the pudding is in the eating and the unhealthy economy and poor history of recent government is clear evidence of the fact that we are not doing a good job. Something has to change, and change means not just for now, but for the future as well. That means not just fixing the system but also putting in place mechanisms that ensure we never, ever get ourselves into this kind of mess again.

And the starting point for that has to be education.

LIFE'S PERPETUAL CONFLICT AND THE PHILOSOPHICAL PENDULUM

One of the hardest things about being human is the balancing act between self-interest and community interest. From birth we are entirely self-motivated, demanding what we need and expecting it immediately. Over time we have to learn that we cannot always get what we want immediately but that's only part of the lesson. We also have to learn that our interests have to dovetail with those of other people. This starts within the family and then spreads outside the home to cover our wider circle: friends, schoolmates, team-mates and so on. But it is always a juggling act and our entire lives are a constant conflict between catering for our own interests and sublimating them to those of others.

Of course this is part and parcel of our survival kit – an essential ingredient of our dependence on, and interdependence with, others. But it is also significant because it means we live with perpetual conflict, for this conflict pervades everything we do. And this conflict has more wide-reaching consequences than we might realise, and not just in the context of how we contribute to a democratic society, but also to how society works as a whole.

I recently came across a theory called "Society's Forty Year Pendulum", which is outlined in a book; 'Pendulum: How Past Generations Shape Our Present and Predict Our Future.'[24] The book seems to support this point as the authors describe the "duality of the 'Me' and the 'We'…" and present and support a theory that says public opinion is driven by the energies of this duality. According to them it is a good thing when each of these balances the other. Unfortunately, because "we always take a good thing too far" we push each to an extreme and thus create an oscillation between the two that creates a forty year cycle. They posit:

---

[24] 'Pendulum: How Past Generations Shape Our Present and Predict Our Future' by Roy H Williams and Michael R Drew Vanguard Press © 2012

"The 'Me' energies are driven by the philosophy of the individual as 'unique, and special and possessing unlimited potential.' The 'Me' values:

- Demand freedom of expression.
- Applaud personal liberty.
- Want to achieve a better life.
- Are about big dreams.
- Desire to be Number One: 'I came, I saw, I conquered.'
- Admire individual confidence and are attracted to decisive people.
- Believe leadership is, 'Look at me. Admire me. Emulate me if you can.'
- Strengthen a society's sense of identity by elevating attractive heroes.

On the other hand the 'We' energies are driven by the philosophy of the group, the team, the tribe, the collective. The 'We' values:

- Demand conformity for the common good.
- Applaud personal responsibility.
- Believe a million men are wiser than one man: 'Two heads are better than one.'
- Want to create a better world.
- Are about small actions.
- Desire to be productive member of the team: 'I came, I saw, I concurred.'
- Admire individual humility and are attracted to thoughtful people.
- Believe leadership is, 'This is the problem as I see it. Please consider the things that I am telling you and perhaps we can solve this problem together.'
- Elevate attractive heroes who strengthen a society's sense of identity.
- Strengthen a society's sense of purpose as it considers all its problems."

Of course, here you are effectively coming back to the earlier question as to whether democracy is actually an impossible ideal; something Thomas Mann pointed out way back when he said, "Logically considered, freedom and equality are mutually exclusive, just as society and the individual are mutually exclusive." Thus it should hardly be any surprise when, according to Williams and Drew these opposite but equal forces create a pendulum that moves from its central balanced position to one extreme over twenty years and then swings back as the opposing values take sway, taking twenty years before starting a twenty-year swing to the opposite extreme, thus moving from one extreme of its oscillation to the other every forty years.

Depicting this as an historical cycle, they maintain that the pendulum was in a central, balanced position in 1963, then swung upward to the "Me" zenith in 1983, returned back to its central position in 2003 (apparently driven by the 'X-Generation) and is now moving toward a "We" zenith.

It certainly is an interesting theory and there is little doubt you could argue strongly for it. The current environment is more "We" focused as a result of the now more clearly apparent consequences of the excesses of the last "Me" cycle. However, personally I would like to see which political parties were in power during these cycles before I was convinced. That is simply because, if you think about it at a different level, you could say that this duality is actually representative of left-wing and right-wing politics, with the left-wing being socialist, we-centric, and the right wing conservative, me-centric. Thus the juxtaposition of the two phenomena would make an interesting comparison and, if there was a correlation, validate the theory more.

However, it is not the validity or otherwise of the theory that matters; rather the premise that lies behind it. Either way, we have to find a way to balance this duality and reduce these duelling energies and the conflict that they fan. We have to continue our quest to make the impossible possible.

The only way we can do it is to have a better education system creating a society of people who recognise the part they have to play, understand the consequences of their decisions and have the capability to make informed, balanced decisions.

"Too many people think that economics is this subject that should wait until the university level. But it can't wait that long."

ROBERT DUVALL

CHAPTER SEVEN
DISECONOMIES OF SCALE

> "Start with the idea that you can't repeal the laws of economics. Even if they are inconvenient."
>
> **LAWRENCE SUMMERS**

The problem with economics is that, whether you like to consider it a science or not (and there are plenty who might argue that it is not[25]) it *is* a science in so far as – just like any science – its laws cannot just be ignored. They may be inconvenient but they will turn around and bite you if you ignore them. If we are to avoid the misfortune of having the government we deserve, we certainly need to have a better understanding of the world around us, and not least of economics.

There is no doubt that we have not being paying the laws of economics their dues. The hard truth is that we would not be in our current economic quandary if we had understood them better. Now, you could debate until the cows come home as to whether we have tried wilfully to repeal them, simply ignored them or just been ignorant of them. Whatever the reason, I believe, once more, that it boils down to the great divide between commerce and economics. Business has too narrow a focus and business leaders do not have the kind of understanding of economics that their positions warrant.

THE EMPIRICAL EVIDENCE

Now you may feel that is rather a controversial statement, so let me support it with some empirical evidence.

I stumbled upon it when I found myself unable to reconcile the current near-record levels of unemployment with the facts that:

---

[25] Even Paul Samuelson, the first economist to win the Nobel Prize, once said, "Economics has never been a science. And it is now even less than a few years ago."

- More people than ever before are *in* employment; and
- Stocks were trading higher than they were before the (2008) financial crisis, which meant they were pretty close to, if not at, an all-time high.

What on earth does that tell us? Perhaps it is an indication that there are too many people: that the world is overpopulated. Yet even if the answer is as simple as that – and I don't think for a moment it is – it is not a problem that is going to go away overnight. In any case I wanted to probe a little deeper, so I took the published annual accounts of one of the world's largest companies and started to analyse them over a ten year period. That is where my misgivings started.

These accounts showed that operating profits had grown by 1.487 billion currency units[26] over the ten years. Pretty impressive, I am sure you will agree. However, during this time – the same ten years – the financial statements showed that the staff costs had **decreased** by 2.014 billion currency units. That means that – as you can see from the diagram which shows the cumulative change (delta) in profits versus the cumulative staff cost savings – the staff cost savings were 136% of the increased profits, due largely to **average employee numbers being reduced by 110,000 people**. (39% of the number at the beginning of the period.)

Of course you cannot blame the directors for this. Their role is to maximise profits and reducing costs is one of only three ways they can do this. Conventional wisdom thus makes it perfectly legitimate for reduced staff costs to be a valid investment criterion. Thus they are quite entitled to claim the credit for this phenomenon and attribute it to their sound investments (implicitly as a result of their unique strategic wisdom, commercial nous and sheer business brilliance, for which this small group personally earned 254 million currency units!) And the accounts are not wrong for disclosing it in this manner.

---

[26] I have used currency units rather than the specific currency deliberately to help ensure that the company cannot be readily identified.

XYZ LIMITED
10 Year Trend: Cumulative Staff Cost Savings vs. Cumulative Change in Profits (Profit Delta)

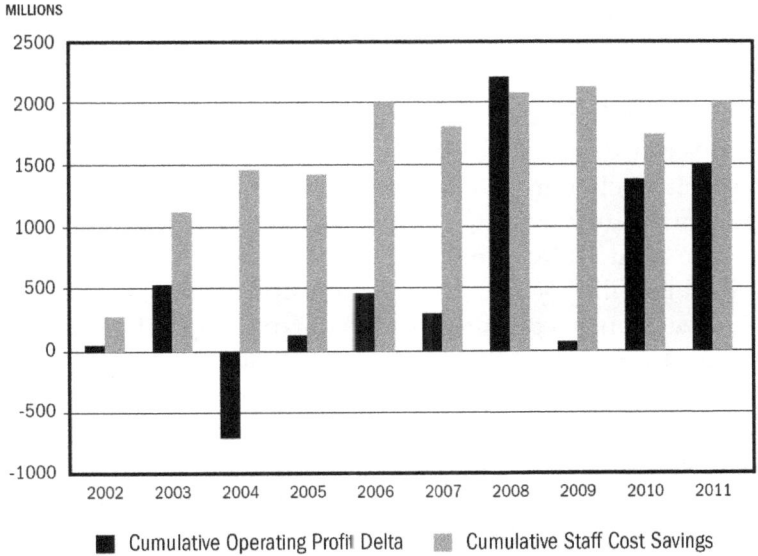

■ Cumulative Operating Profit Delta　■ Cumulative Staff Cost Savings

Now accounts can no more lie than statistics – despite what Disraeli said about there being three types of distortion of the truth – "lies, damned lies and statistics." At the very most you could describe accounts as a form of statistics. All they do is provide a snapshot history of a series of transactions, which are independently audited and certified. It is only how they are used that determines their effect for better or worse. As ever this is a matter of interpretation and, in the case of financial statements, the result of adherence to convention.

After all, I managed to complete this analysis using only what I could glean from the published, audited annual financial statements with their accompanying notes and reports. But it was a time consuming exercise and I had to dig. So you have to ask if the accounts are giving a one-sided perspective of things? Are they wrong by omission for not including this kind of analysis?

THE ECONOMIC AND COMMERCIAL DICHOTOMY

Once again it boils down to the divide between commerce and economics. Conventional wisdom says commercially it is always right to minimise costs even if it is at the expense of people, but **economically, putting people out of work only transfers costs – it does not reduce them**. Thus, ignoring the more conventional arguments about the demoralising, destabilising and depressing effects of laying people off and the inevitable decline in productivity through reduced employee engagement as a result, one has to question the long-term wisdom of such decisions. It is an approach that jeopardises the sustainability of both the business and society.

Convention says that it is by maximising efficiency (as measured by profitability) that a business optimises its contribution to society. Thus traditionalists argue that a business meets its dues to society through the taxes it pays. Unfortunately, you saw earlier tax avoidance has become an industry in its own right and it is not just wealthy people who do not pay their full share of taxes. In the UK there was outrage following the news that major organisations such as Amazon, Google and Starbucks barely paid any taxes at all, despite the enormous profits they had made in the country. All of which means that such job losses have a significantly negative effect on the wider economy.

This phenomenon is not restricted to the UK. The whole practice of off-shoring has become *de rigueur* in many developed countries. The net effect of this is that jobs move to low cost locations elsewhere in the world, often with the arrangement sweetened by favourable tax incentives that help to improve the returns even more. This may seem to be sound policy at the micro-economic level, but it leaves the displaced people looking for alternative work. This means that at the macro-economic level the transfer of jobs amounts to nothing more than a transfer of costs. The economy as a whole is only better off if the displaced workers can find equivalent or better jobs.

Here conventional wisdom comes to the fore once more, by claiming that the country is still better off, as the profits are repatriated and either paid out in dividends or else reinvested in new growth opportunities, which does more long-term good. Conventional wisdom may also even be used to reinforce those arguments by claiming that this foreign reinvestment is good because it follows the Henry Ford example and creates jobs and, therefore, wealth in these other countries, which then creates a market beneficial to the home economy. Thus it is not only morally right in opening up and developing these poorer nations, but it is also "good for us" and therefore is a perfect win-win.

This may, however, be where the laws of economics are being flouted. My analysis, remember, showed that 110,000 jobs had been shed by this one company over the past ten years. If this was the result of off-shoring, those jobs would have moved, not been lost. No company can shed 39% of its workforce through off-shoring alone. Admittedly this is just the analysis of one set of accounts, but do you really think it would be that different in any other?

In fact you possibly don't even have to conduct such analyses to know that this is representative of a worldwide phenomenon. Just look at your own experience, or your own organisation and you can see it for yourself. The likelihood is that you have probably experienced redundancy first hand, and even if you haven't, you are likely to have witnessed it happen to others or listened to the news where job-losses are an almost daily announcement.

Conventional wisdom will cry out that this is not the result of callous executives but simply the inevitable result of our massive technological progress. It is simply the price that businesses have to pay in order to remain competitive and increase their profits sufficiently to survive.

That may be so, and I wouldn't try to refute that. The fact remains, however, that you have 110,000 workers displaced from one company. Multiply that across a number of companies and the whole marketplace and the whole community and you can begin to see why we have a problem; one that we are blindly ignoring. Of course, (as you will have guessed by now) I am talking about the diseconomies of scale.

Now you are probably very familiar with the concept of economies of scale. These occur when more units of a good or a service can be produced on a larger scale, with less input costs, resulting in a lower marginal or per unit cost. Originally identified by Adam Smith as the result of the division of labour and increased specialisation, this was first fully exploited by Henry Ford with his production line, which led to mass production in almost all manufacturing. A more recent example in a completely different context was Sam Walton and Walmart, with his bulk buying philosophy of "stack 'em high and sell 'em cheap."

Rather ironically, considering all the other Henry Ford lessons that they seem to have been forgotten, business executives have latched on to the concept of economies of scale and pursued it with an exemplary dedication, determination and vigour. Unfortunately, in the process they have completely forgotten that there is a corresponding opposite law too.

This can be illustrated by the following diagram.

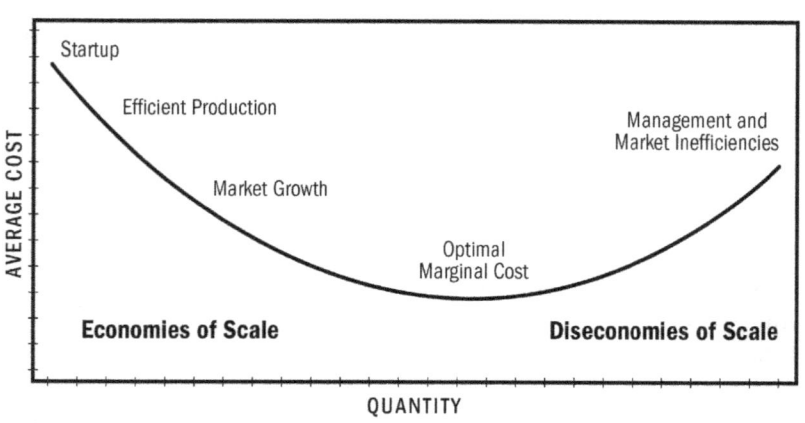

Diseconomies of scale happen when organisations get too big. There are a number of examples of where this happens and what gives rise to it. Some examples include:

- Poor communication as a result of more people being involved and information failing to flow through the organisation as it should.
- Co-ordination problems, where the communication may actually be working well, but the ability to schedule the necessary resources at precisely the right time becomes difficult.
- Disengaged, de-motivated and demoralised staff who feel they are just "a number" and thus lose any sense of pride in their work. In extreme cases where the work is too mundane or tedious this can actually lead to workers deliberately sabotaging the systems.
- Mergers and acquisitions, where different corporate cultures clash and resentments fester and grow.

The list can go on, but whatever the issues, they create a headache for management, particularly mergers and acquisitions where research appears to indicate that anything between 50% and 85% fail. According to a CBS News report[27] "one KPMG study found that 83% of these deals hadn't boosted shareholder returns, while a separate study by A.T. Kearney concluded that total returns on M&A were negative." It is hardly any wonder then that, in querying why they persist, the report continues, "They're glamorous, high-profile, and make vast amounts of money for intermediaries. They feed CEO vanity and a love of size. They also persist because they are often decided by rank-and-file shareholders, who are those at the furthest remove from the company's operations. Those with the most power are also those with the least insight."

If you doubt the research you only have to look at the 2007 acquisition of Alcan by Rio Tinto for $38.1 billion. By the beginning of 2013 Rio Tinto had been compelled to write-off $25 billion of those costs. Now this write-off happens to correspond to the premium that analysts reckon that Rio Tinto

---

[27] http://www.cbsnews.com/8301-505125_162-57411239/why-mergers-fail/ 23 April 2012

paid for the acquisition, but whether that is fact, coincidence or just the backward arithmetical calculation of the write-off, the fact remains that a CEO's willingness to pay a 65% premium suggests that the deal was more of a macho "mine's-bigger-than-yours" competition than a rational commercial exchange. The CEO has now stepped down, but this is just an example of how easily executives can get carried away, sweep any potential naysayers aside and act in a way that self-evidently is not in their shareholders' best interests.

Perhaps in view of what we saw earlier about the widening wealth gap, mergers are also a way to justify massive pay rises for the people at the top. What is really amazing, though, is how they manage to convince the share-holders whose votes in favour are rather like turkeys voting for Thanksgiving or Christmas.

All mergers, however, are specific to the company and are therefore commercial. Mergers are also a classic method of disposing of excessive profit to reduce or avoid tax liabilities, while at the same time increasing the (apparent) net worth of the overall business and thus increase shareholder dividend payments. Despite the fact that there is, "continuing evidence that the majority of mergers and acquisitions actually destroy, rather than create, value,"[28] mergers persist and thrive. They take no account of the macro-economic effects we have been looking at, which suggest the damage may be even greater than we thought. These make the diseconomies of scale even larger and more significant.

Record employment and record unemployment simultaneously provide the evidence of this. They also provide evidence that as a society we have to change. We cannot continue in this manner. We have to think of new approaches to management and how we account for our people. Ultimately it boils down to a question of sustainability.

---

[28] Source: Paper entitled: Beyond Default: Moving Your Organisation to an Improved Future" by David Trafford of Formicio Limited Published 22 November 2012. http://formicio.com/index.php/archives/5077

SUSTAINABILITY – A WIDER PERSPECTIVE ON A GREATER PRIORITY

It has become fashionable whenever the word 'sustainability' is used to think about it in terms of the environment. Sustainability is, however, about so much more than just "being green." For starters a business has to be sustainable if it going to continue to fulfil its purpose in the community. Yet how many businesses actually look at their sustainability?

Just think about my analysis of XYZ Limited for a moment. That seems to suggest that over ten years the increase in profitability was made up entirely of savings in people costs. (What else does the fact that these were 136% of the increased profitability over the period tell you?) Now, you can bet your bottom dollar that this group was investing billions in other activities intended to grow the business. So where are the returns on those investments? If they are delivering what they are supposed to deliver (and hopefully management does manage, measure and ensure this) then there have to be a number of other areas where the company is losing money at an incredible rate. In other words there have to be some massive commercial diseconomies of scale that the executive are failing to recognise, respond to or – most significantly – to repair. So just how sustainable is this business?

It would appear that with the current scale of operations and standard of accounting that it could continue operating indefinitely. However, there is very real possibility that this could only be because (rather like the banks) it has exceeded a critical mass and become too big to fail, and the sheer scale of its operations will allow it to continue operating the way it is. There is, however, also a chance that – like the Lehman Brothers of this world – something, sometime in the future could cause it collapse overnight.

That latter danger is increased by the very situation it is helping to create. If companies like this all continue to reduce employee numbers at such a rate, then the unemployment problem will never be solved: the economy will continue to decline and the market shrink, creating a continuous downward spiral that will erode its very ability to sell its products. In fact if companies like this continue to operate in the way they are you could make a case for that outcome becoming inevitable, and the key question becoming not if, but when.

So, if we are to be serious about sustainability, we must think more economically and not just commercially. That means organisations need to consider Corporate Social Responsibility (CSR) more widely and broaden their definition of the term to include their responsibility to their employees as citizens of the communities in which they operate.

"The animals that depend on instinct have an inherent knowledge of the laws of economics and how to apply them. Man; with his powers of reason, has reduced economics to a level of a farce." James Thurber

If this farce is not to turn into a tragedy we need to look more comprehensively at the way we do things. Of all people, perhaps Vivienne Westwood summed it up best when she said, "Economists treat economics as if it is a pure science divorced from the facts of life. The result of this false accountancy is a wilful confusion under cover of which industry wreaks havoc scot-free and ignores the environmental cost." This demands of us to look at both sides of the coin in the way we have started to here and, strange as it may seem, perhaps accounting can actually lead the way!

CHAPTER EIGHT
SABOTAGING THE STATE

> "The government, which was designed for the people, has got into the hands of the bosses and their employers, the special interests. An invisible empire has been set up above the forms of democracy."
>
> **WOODROW WILSON**

Some things never change! It is around a hundred years since Woodrow Wilson made that observation. It is such a pity that greater attention has not been paid to such people for, in retrospect, his words look almost prophetic.

Of course there have always been cynics who accuse government of being controlled by big business and it is certainly one of the first cries of criticism when people disagree with a government decision. However, their concerns are not entirely unjustified when one looks at the amount of lobbying that goes on, with a whole industry built around the practice. When you add the whole issue of political funding into the mix it certainly does become a grey area. How can you ever be sure that politicians are acting "for" the people – in their best interests, rather than the politician's own?

This question becomes even more relevant when you factor in the size of government and its inexorable growth over the past hundred years. This scale of growth demands financing. Remember, governments do not produce. So in order to grow in the way they have, they have had to develop ways of funding that growth and there are only two, and governments all over the world have become adept at both:

- Raising tax revenues
- Borrowing more

Both come at a price!

THE INVISIBLE EMPIRE - REVEALED

Much as it would like to, government cannot just raise taxes at will – especially in a democracy – because to do so risks raising the ire of the people and thereby reduces their chances of re-election. Consequently, they can normally only do so in very small increments or by identifying new forms of tax; the so-called "stealth taxes." (The only time this does not apply is when there is a crisis and they are then able to convince the people that there is no alternative and "it is all for their own good!" Unfortunately, as things currently stand, it looks awfully like we could be heading in that direction in the not too distant future.)

Let's just ignore, however, the question of how government levies tax for a moment and focus on the source of that tax.

A significant proportion of government's tax comes from corporate taxpayers and especially the large companies. Logically, this means that the better a business does – the more profit it makes – the more tax it will pay. As a result both "big business" and government stand to do well when the business does well. This is significant because it in turn means that they actually have a common interest and consequently it dilutes and even negates the supervisory, overseeing role that government is expected to play. That is possibly the primary reason the financial services industry was allowed to get away with all it did in the lead-up to the 2008 financial crisis. Critics bemoan the poor regulatory role played by government, and claim that this was a major factor in the lead up to the crisis. Maybe it was, but the fact is that it suited governments to let the banks keep making super-profits and it was perhaps naïve to expect otherwise.

So Wilson was completely right when he talked about an "invisible empire set up above the forms of democracy." Even so, however, the concept might not be so bad if everything remained in balance and continued to work as it should, with everyone playing their part. Unfortunately, as with most relationships, one party tends to dominate, and this means the system loses its equilibrium and then the structure starts to crumble and head towards collapse, which is precisely what is happening; the system is on the verge of collapse.

THE TAX CONUNDRUM

All things being equal the systems should continue to work as long as business sticks to its side of the bargain and pays its taxes. Unfortunately, as you have already seen this is not what has been happening.

Tax revenues from corporations are in fact reducing on three broad inter-connected and hard to separate fronts:

- Tax avoidance;
- Off-shoring; and
- Down-sizing.

TAX AVOIDANCE

We saw earlier how Barclays Bank has been part of an entire industry specialising in helping other organisations and wealthy people take advantage of loopholes in the tax laws and reduce their tax liabilities. Remember their billion pound profits from this activity? It is impossible to speculate how much this cost the UK Exchequer, but it has to be a multiple of many times that number.

Firstly, that's because the money their clients paid to them would have been turnover (revenue) to the bank before it deducted any expenses. Secondly, because the expenses deducted from that turnover to yield those profits are likely to have been significant. After all, it takes a number of highly qualified, highly creative and highly paid people to trawl through the thousands of pages of tax legislation to discover where there were weaknesses and then to conceive of the kind of complicated and devious machinations to exploit them. So to make the kinds of profits it did, Barclays must have charged a significant amount.

The truly frightening aspect of all this, however, is that Barclays is only one of a number of organisations that were working this "industry." Factor in the competitor banks, and the "Big Four" accounting firms alone and the numbers are likely to be mind-blowing.

OFF-SHORING

Off-shoring is the relocation of jobs to other countries where labour is plentiful, reasonably well educated and considerably less expensive. This trend has been going on for decades and has been widely recognised, with the drastic and widespread reduction of the manufacturing industry, as a contributor to the state of the economy (and, in the UK at least, the – very ironical – emphasis placed on financial services and the position of London as a "world centre" of the financial services industry.) Even leading entrepreneurs like James Dyson moved all their manufacturing off-shore because that is the only way to make products at a price low enough to compete in a global economy because – with the justification that all parents loathe – "everyone else is doing it too!"

On a global scale this may be the good thing that it is claimed to be because it does give the less-developed countries the chance to grow and develop. Certainly, there seems to be some merit in such moves because they follow Henry Ford's principles and create an enlarged market that might not otherwise exist. Whether the profits returned, however, are enough to compensate for the jobs lost and the consequent tax revenues forgone as a result, is highly debatable. You saw in the last chapter that corporations like Amazon, Google and Starbucks are making huge profits in the UK, but hardly paying any taxes. That is a direct consequence of off-shoring, foreign ownership and increasingly global change and is a real problem – especially when you factor in the afore-mentioned industrial-scale tax avoidance.

DOWN-SIZING

In Chapter Seven I illustrated how a world-leading, international corporation had reduced its employee numbers by 110,000 people over the past ten years, and how that fact alone, with the related reduction in staff costs, had more than accounted for their growth in profits. That is 110,000 people who, unless they found replacement positions that paid the same or more, would end up paying less income tax. So here again you have a potentially disastrous and definitely debilitating effect on the national tax revenues.

Conventional wisdom argues that these shifts simply demand a re-skilling of the work-force due to the changing nature of the work required, and that this is simply "the invisible hand" of the market compelling this evolution. As I pointed out before, however, the widespread increase in the numbers of unemployed people would suggest that this is a largely fallacious argument, and that the re-skilling is not actually happening. Consequently, tax revenues will definitely be depleted and tax rates will have to rise and/or new sources of revenue be found.

CALAMITOUS CONSEQUENCES

While in some areas businesses may be pushing the envelope as far as they legitimately dare, these practices are not illegal. In fact they comply with what conventional wisdom describes as sound commercial sense. These three strategies, nevertheless, combine to create a triple whammy. They all feed off one another and serve to compound the depletion of the government's revenues, compelling government to try to find other sources to compensate. As we know, the only way the government can feasibly do so is to increase taxes or to borrow more.

With borrowing out of the question that only leaves raising taxes. Unfortunately in doing this the Government has to tap into an already hard hit taxpayer base, which creates a vicious cycle because it has a further eroding effect on the economy at large. As a result, in the longer term there is likely to be an inevitable decline in the economic prosperity of the nation as a whole. Indeed this is precisely what is already happening throughout Europe, only governments are not being honest and are continuing to rely on historic solutions that no longer work and cannot work.

Thus such actions by business, because they are so damaging to the economy where the business is domiciled, fall way outside the definition of good corporate social responsibility. Possibly even more significant, however, is the fact that they are ultimately detrimental to the long term sustainability of the business itself. After all, as Henry Ford demonstrated, if there is no thriving economy, there is no thriving market.

THE BORROWING CONUNDRUM

While raising taxes is not necessarily anathema to any government it is not something that will endear it to its citizens. Of course that is a problem when it is those citizens – in their role as voters – who keep the Government in power (or not, as the case may be.) Consequently you once more have a situation where your leaders are not actually acting as leaders and governments have tended to avoid raising taxes and instead resorted to borrowing wherever possible.

Ever since Roosevelt's "New Deal", economic practice has been for governments to borrow money to spend more in order to stimulate growth. What was new in Roosevelt's day became the conventional wisdom. Thus in tough economic times both government and the electorate look to increased government spending to ride to the rescue and reignite the economy. It is now the expectation, and the survival of both is considered to depend on it.

Unfortunately, as any householder borrower knows, debt comes at a price *and* has to be repaid. Even more unfortunately this is something that governments universally either do not know, do not understand or have wilfully ignored. That is why the debt crisis has reached almost epidemic proportions as governments all over the world, but particularly in Europe and the US, teeter on the verge of bankruptcy, unable to repay the vast sums they have borrowed and unable to borrow any more simply because the interest payments have become unaffordable.

In the UK, government debt when the Coalition government came to power in 2010 stood at £700 billion; by the time of the next election that debt is forecast to have *doubled*. In other words – **despite the tax hikes and austerity measures that have the people protesting and striking** – the debt will be £1.4 trillion.[29] If the words are too difficult to absorb perhaps this chart will make the point!

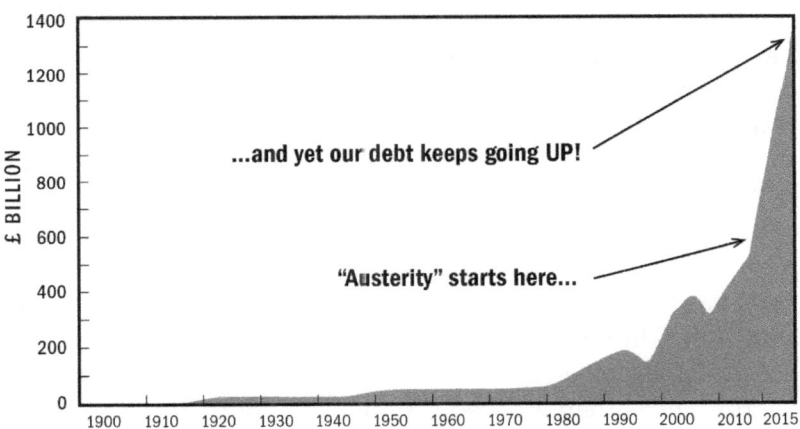

This is a truly frightening picture, and it follows on from Iceland, Ireland, Portugal, Spain, Greece and Cyprus. In Cyprus you had the situation of the parliament initially refusing the European Union bailout terms because it included taking 10% of the depositors' funds directly from their bank accounts. The final deal ended up taking 20% from every depositor's account with more than €100,000 in what effectively amounted to virtually unannounced, immediate tax. That's the real problem, because – when push comes to shove – it is the citizens who have to pay the price.

---

[29] Source: Moneyweek Ltd, Registered Office: 8th Floor, Friars Bridge Court, 41-45 Blackfriars Road, London SE1 8NZ. © 2013 MoneyWeek Ltd

The US is hardly any better. There the national debt is running at over $16.7 trillion! Not only is this the highest debt of any single country but it is also more than 100% of GDP, which puts it in much the same league as the major European debtor nations.[30]

It may be worthwhile pointing out here that of this $16.7 trillion, $11.9 trillion (71.2%) is classified as public debt; the remaining $4.8 trillion is classified as "Intra-governmental Holdings." As the term implies this is money that is owed by the government to itself, and held as Government Account securities. Apparently most of this is owed to Social Security and other trust funds, which were running surpluses. In other words, as I saw it described somewhere, the government has been making out IOUs to itself. In any event these securities are a promise to repay these funds when Baby Boomers retire over the next twenty years, and are, consequently, very much a potential time bomb. In any event the interest on the debt was a whopping $454 billion in 2011, despite interest rates being at an all-time low, and is currently budgeted at $248 billion, the sixth largest budget item.[31]

What is particularly frightening is that shortly after President Bill Clinton left office there was a surplus in this account, which means that this entire debt has accumulated in slightly more than a decade. While this could also be seen as an encouraging indicator that it is not as big a problem as it might appear on the surface, that is unlikely to be the case. The sheer scale of the debt and the fact that it is such a big proportion of GDP makes it a very serious problem.

So what has given rise to this phenomenal debt spike? Unfortunately, on the surface it looks very easy to explain. President George W Bush created a deficit of $3.3 billion largely as a result of 9/11 and the subsequent "War on Terror" which added $600-800 billion a year to the defence budget, while President Obama added a further $5.1 billion as a re-

---

[30] Source: US Treasury
http://www.treasurydirect.gov/NP/BPDLogin?application=np as at 29/3/2013
[31] Source: About.com US Economy March 2013

sult of those continuing defence costs, as well as his economic stimulus measures to deal with the 2008 financial crisis, amongst other things.[32]

ECONOMIC TREACHERY

So with most of Europe, the UK and the US all having levels of debt that are no longer sustainable it seems clear why borrowing is no longer an option for any government. Consequently the strategies and actions of business leaders are not only short-sighted, but can be said to be treacherous to the extent that they sabotage the economy in which the business is domiciled and betray the business stakeholders. They compound an already dangerous situation and are partly responsible for the decline in living standards currently being felt by so much of the developed world.

Yet, despite the rioting and the protests, very few seem to recognise the danger. Conventional wisdom keeps us buying into the old models and paradigms, and the systems that have evolved out of them appear to be too rigid and complicated for anyone to conceive of changing them. Consequently the invisible empire continues to thrive, and we all stand by as it equally invisibly erodes everything that past generations have built up and all they have lived and died for.

You have to admit, however, that it is all very confusing. If the banks are bust and having to be rescued by governments, which are themselves technically bankrupt, you have to ask yourself, "Where the hell is all the money?" I am afraid it will take somebody smarter than me to answer that definitely. I do, however, have a pretty shrewd idea (and the widening wealth gap might be a good clue!)

---

[32] Ibid http://useconomy.about.com/od/usdebtanddeficit/p/US-Debt-by-President.htm

SABOTAGING THE STATE

CHAPTER NINE
THE EMPEROR'S NEW CLOTHES

"But he isn't wearing anything at all!"
FROM 'THE EMPEROR'S NEW SUIT' BY HANS CHRISTIAN ANDERSEN

The story of the emperor's new suit has been translated into over 100 languages and is well known throughout the world. So you are probably familiar with how it tells of a young lad who is the only one with the temerity to state the obvious and so expose the stupidity and sycophancy that made a whole scam possible. That was only a fairy tale, but today we may be dealing with a real life scenario that is even more breath-taking in its scale.

Now if you wanted to be ironic you could say perhaps our susceptibility is excusable. After all, if there is an invisible empire then it seems entirely logical that there should be an invisible emperor who is wearing an invisible suit. Unfortunately there is no place for such irony, with the consequences being so much more serious than merely embarrassed royalty. Let's explore just how exposed we are.

It all starts with governments' need to raise revenue. You have already seen that the only two avenues for doing this – raising taxes and borrowing – are not the most attractive options for any government in tough economic times. The first is likely to jeopardise their chances of re-election and so ensure their loss of power, while the second is virtually impossible. Consequently they have been desperate to find a "third way" and it appears that they may have found it with Quantitative Easing (QE).

The problem is that while the concepts of increased taxes and increased borrowing are relatively simple and, therefore, easy to understand, QE is more complex and, for the likes of simple people like me, very hard to get to grips with. Let me, however, attempt to explain it and what my concerns are.

GETTING TO GRIPS WITH QUANTITATIVE EASING

Broadly "Quantitative Easing" (QE) is an unconventional monetary policy used by the central bank to stimulate the economy when interest rates are very low and standard monetary policy has become ineffective. This entails the central bank buying financial assets, thus creating notional money and injecting a pre-determined quantity of it into the economy. Generally, these purchases are conducted on a credit basis, so no real money changes hands.

The financial assets purchased are mortgage-backed securities from commercial banks and other private institutions, along with the tradable and negotiable debt obligations issued by a country's government, which are known as Treasuries. Commercial banks can then use the central bank's credit to make more loans. This enables them to stimulate demand by giving businesses more money to expand, and shoppers more credit with which to buy things – which, as I am sure you will recall, are the very things that caused the economic crisis in the first place!

QE stimulates the economy in another way. The central government auctions off large quantities of Treasuries to pay for growth policies. As the central bank buys Treasuries, it increases demand, keeping Treasury yields low. Since Treasuries are the basis for all long-term interest rates, it also keeps auto, furniture and other consumer debt rates affordable. The same is true for corporate bonds, allowing businesses to expand more cheaply. Most important, QE keeps mortgage rates low and that's important to support the housing market.

Furthermore, by increasing the money supply, QE keeps the value of the currency low. This makes stocks seem like a relatively good investment to foreign investors, and exports relatively cheaper. Sounds good, apart from the fact that every major economy in Europe, as well as the US is in the same boat and doing the same thing! (Not to mention the problems, which develop when a country starts to import excessively because it no longer manufactures or exports very much!)

Now I don't know about you, but this all sounds like a massive con trick to me. Here you have a government rescuing banks by lending them 'money' that it doesn't have, in order that they can continue to lend money at low interest rates to an already over-indebted population.

If that is not bad enough, this same over-indebted population is – as we have witnessed from the situations in Europe where the chickens have already come home to roost – the bank of last resort. Consequently, if QE should prove to be a failure it is we who will pay the price. So how likely is that?

Of course that is a how-long-is-a-piece-of-string type of question, complicated by the fact that you are dealing with the future which is always uncertain. You would, however, have to think the risks are closely aligned to the debt situation, which, from what we have seen of that situation, means that they are high. Thus the overarching issue here has to be the effect that QE has on the debt.

Well, as best I can understand the way QE works, it appears that QE is not included in national debt figures and does not add to the government debt. On the contrary, it may be that it even reduces it. See if you can figure this out because frankly I can't.

The mechanics of QE seem to work as follows:

1. A nation's central bank announces that it will engage in QE – that it will buy x billions of currency from banks.
2. The government's treasury issues long-term bonds to finance the government debt.
3. The banks, now knowing the central bank is a ready buyer for those bonds, buy the bonds directly from the government treasury.
4. The banks either sell the bonds on the market to individual and corporate investors or sell them to the central bank at a small premium.
5. The central bank then creates a deposit in the reserve accounts of those banks for the amount of bonds it is buying from the banks plus the small premium. The money deposited never existed before. It does not

come out of some other account. It is just a batch of very large numbers suddenly created as deposits in the reserve accounts of those banks. (Reserve accounts being money that national banks must by law keep in reserve to meet the capital fund requirements demanded by law.) Instantly, each of those banks is billions of dollars richer.

6. The central bank then takes possession of the bonds and becomes the government's bond holder.

In the end, of course, the central bank is still the primary buyer of debt because the banks would not be buying the bonds in such number if they did not know the central bank was willing to buy any that they were not able to resell to private investors at an attractive profit. *In other words the central bank is underwriting this debt.*

Now as the central bank is ostensibly an independent body, operating at arm's-length of government, you could argue that this figure is not technically a part of government debt. At the end of the day, however, the central bank is owned by the government or, at the very least – if the worst came to the worst – would have to have its debts covered by government. Consequently, you could argue that the government is certainly adding to its liability and that this figure should be added to its debt.

But ...

There are others who argue that because the government owns the central bank this figure can actually be *deducted* from the national debt. As best I understand it, the argument for this is that the government is not creating new debt through this process but is actually buying back existing debt. This is illustrated in the following table downloaded from a website called Tax Research UK and created by an extremely reputable economic expert, Richard Murphy[33], based on data from the Bank of England and HM Treasury.

---

[33] Source: http://www.taxresearch.org.uk/Blog/2012/07/13/the-untold-truth-about-quantitative-easing-is-it-simply-cancels-debt-and-that-means-national-debt-is-now-just-45-1-of-gdp/

HOW QUANTITATIVE EASING REDUCES NATIONAL DEBT

	2008-09 £ BILLION	2009-10 £ BILLION	2010-11 £ BILLION	2011-12 £ BILLION	CUMULATIVE £ BILLION
Additional Debt Issued	79.6	153.5	145.0	117.8	495.9
Quantitative Easing (QE)		-200.0		-125.0	-325.0
Actual Net New Debt	79.6	-46.5	145.0	-7.2	170.9

Debt at 2007-08	527.2
Gross Additional Debt	495.9
Reported Debt 2011-12	1023.1
Less QE	325.0
Actual Net Debt	698.1
Reported Ratio of Debt to GDP	66.10%
Actual Ratio of Debt to GDP	45.10%
Ratio of Debt to GDP in 2007-08	36.70%

As I say, I really have no idea how to call it. I don't even know if these figures are the ones actually being used. It seems to me, however, that it must be something like this that enables the people in charge of national finances to even sleep at night. Even so you have to wonder if this whole QE approach is being led by our modern equivalent of the tailors in Hans Christian Anderson's fairy tale.

The risks associated with Quantitative Easing

Generally the perceived risks associated with QE are:

- That it does not actually stimulate the economy because people are so indebted that they don't actually want to borrow more.
- That banks and investors take the money being made available and use it to buy assets like shares and commodities, rather than lending it for more productive purposes like business development.
- The inevitable risk of inflation from putting more money into circulation.

I would suggest that the second point is very much what has happened given the record stock exchange levels that followed these initiatives. I would also suggest that the inflation risk is possibly considerably higher than our economic policy wonks would have us believe.

For starters, historic precedent shows that countries that have resorted to this technique in the past have fuelled hyper-inflation. The obvious examples are Weimar Germany and Zimbabwe. Our leaders are telling us that this is different; their intentions are not the same and they are not "monetizing debt" in the way attempted by those countries. That, however, is a different spin on the popular definition of insanity as "doing the same thing over and over and expecting a different result!"[34] A different intention does not mean the results of a given action will be different!

Furthermore, they justify their position by pointing to the fact that interest rates are at all-time lows. The problem with that argument is that they have been at these lows for several years now and cannot remain there indefinitely. In fact, given the level of debts that we have been looking at, it is highly unlikely that they will remain at these levels for very much longer. Lenders will soon start looking for higher rates of return given the increased level of risk and once interest rates start rising they will create a vicious cycle of rising costs that will make King Canute look wise.

In fact comparisons to King Canute may be apt, because QE was apparently also tried by Japan when their economy first tanked and as yet, over a decade later, there is nothing to suggest that it worked there. Consequently you cannot help but suspect that our leaders simply don't have any idea of what to do and are simply "playing for time" with their fingers crossed.

---

[34] This quote "Insanity is repeating the same mistakes and expecting different results" appears in the Basic Text of Narcotics Anonymous which was copyrighted in 1982 and later published in 1983. It is found on page 11 of the final "Review Form" which was distributed to the fellowship in November of 1981. It is found on page 23 of the current sixth edition.

FOOTING THE BILL

That brings us back to the Emperor's suit. It seems that our leaders are no less foolish than that fabled emperor. The suit that they are wearing is no less imaginary or more substantial than his. Unfortunately, while his subjects were able to smirk surreptitiously at his self-aggrandizement and delusion because it had no immediate or direct consequences for them, we are not so fortunate.

At the end of the day it is the citizens, the ordinary people, who have to foot the bill, through a significantly lower standard of living as a result of any or all of the following:

- Higher taxes;
- Greatly eroded pensions;
- Higher interest rates that will naturally follow when the lenders recognise the risk of lending to bankrupt governments;
- Higher prices as a result of the inflation caused by all the money that has been created without anything behind it to sustain its value.

As we have seen this is already starting to happen in Europe in countries like Greece, Spain, Portugal, Italy and Cyprus. Other countries, including the UK and US, are likely to be following suit sometime in the not too distant future. The fact is that our systems have proved to be flawed, inadequate and even downright destructive. We have fallen into the trap of conventional wisdom and, like the Emperor, have been conceited, complacent and conned!

Fortunately, (or unfortunately if you enjoy sleeping at night) the spell of invisibility is starting to wear off and the empire is being revealed! You have seen how debt is rising and yet neither governments nor banks have enough money. You have seen how government can create money virtually at will, which effectively increases the "money supply" even though it debases the value of currency. This inflation, arguably, might not actually affect real wealth at the end of the day. However, it certainly enables those who are able to get their hands on it to become wealthier, and you have seen how the wealth gap is widening inexorably, which means that it has to be to the wealthy minority that the "money" is going.

This hardly conforms to the principles of democracy on which modern society was supposed to have been built. Indeed you could argue that we are in danger of destroying the middle class which has been the backbone of modern society and so returning to the inequality of feudal times, with the real wealth – and power – being in the hands of a fortunate, favoured few. That's the scenario that gave rise to the French Revolution in the first place, so if we are to avoid a future revolution, it is time to go back to the drawing board and start afresh. We have no option.

One of my favourite quotes is, quite appropriately, from a Frenchman, Antoine de Saint-Exupery, who said; "As for the future, ours is not to foresee it, but to enable it." The only thing certain about the future is that there is one. We are the ones who shape it. It is up to us.

So far, what I have described enables us to foresee a future and it is not a pleasant prospect. It is certainly not the kind of future we would like our children and grandchildren to inherit. Consequently it is up to us to enable a better one. Hopefully the ideas in the rest of this book will give us a good launching pad to enable a better future!

PART TWO
OVERARCHING PRINCIPLES

CHAPTER TEN
BUILDING ON PRINCIPLES

> "It is a thing of no great difficulty to raise objections against another man's oratory, nay, it is a very easy matter; but to produce better in its place is a work extremely troublesome."
>
> **PLUTARCH**

It is always easy to criticise. Any fool can find fault, and all we have done up until now is to look at what is wrong with the world. The time has come to move out of the company of fools! If we are to enable a better future we need to move beyond finding fault, and instead devise solutions. However, as Plutarch says, that is easier said than done. So how do we move to the next stage and start developing solutions?

For me the starting point, as implied in Chapter Five, has to be principles.

You will recall from there the conversation attributed to HG Wells and Isadora Duncan and how quickly it sparked anger. While it is a delightfully amusing story, it serves to illustrate a more profound point. When HG Wells asked Isadora Duncan if she would sleep with him for a million pounds and she said yes, he had effectively established that she was not averse to the idea. You could say that he had established a principle that she was available. Consequently, when they started "haggling over price" Duncan had no legitimate grounds for getting angry, because she had already sacrificed the moral high ground.

Her statement, "What kind of lady do you think I am?" contains an implicit recognition that what was being proposed was contrary to the general standards of behaviour of the kind of person she saw herself to be, or aspired to be, or by which she wished to be seen. Yet the principle that; "a lady would not do such a thing," had already been discarded in her answer to the first question.

In this instance the proximity of the discussion was so close to the principle that no reasonable response to Wells' reply was possible. In general conversation over the course of time, however, matters generally get further and further removed from principles, and thus discussions get more protracted and arguments can ensue. Indeed Duncan's position perhaps typifies most arguments, for if you analyse them more deeply, they are actually more about policy issues – the how-much-is-it-worth type questions –than issues of principle.

Nowhere is this more apparent than in politics where the passage of time is compounded by the overlay of different measures introduced by alternating parties, as they exercise their temporary grip on power and try to shape things according to their own party policies, while maintaining some sort of continuity. In Chapter Five we explored some of the problems that this has caused but let me give a clearer idea of how society is getting more and more polarised, while moving further and further away from the principles that underpin policy.

Perhaps one of the greatest threats to democracy today is the threat of fundamentalism. Now I am not talking here about the jihadist Islamic threat that "the west" is facing, although that is threat enough in itself and may, in part, be a consequence of our shortcomings as a society. Rather I am talking about the different and more generic form of fundamentalism – a kind of single-issue perspective that becomes dogma and that is making society increasingly intolerant, violent and undemocratic. You can immediately come up with several examples here that highlight the issue:

- The pro-life movement whose extreme members fire-bomb abortion clinics and threaten and kill people who work there. These people are so fanatical that they cannot see that their actions are no different to those they are attacking.

- The pro-gun lobby that demand their right to weapons and see every attempt to reduce the bloodshed these weapons cause as an attack on their constitutional rights.
- The fundamentalist Christians who – despite the basic teachings of the Master Christian who was unable to separate the second great commandment "to love thy neighbour as thyself" from the first "to love the Lord thy God with all thy heart and with all thy soul and with all thy mind":[35]
    - Strongly oppose the ordination of women clergy;
    - Fight against same-sex 'marriage'; and even
    - Burn the Koran, even though doing so is a flagrant disregard of the Golden Rule, to "do unto others as you would have them do unto you" and, therefore, something to which they would take great exception if anyone were to burn the Bible.
- The atheists who, taking exception to what they see as the forcing of religious beliefs upon them and the proselytising of the churches, are just as strident, or even more so, in spreading their non-belief.
- The biggest rift of all: the conservative versus socialist divide. Not only has this divided the world to such an extent that it has very nearly brought it to the brink of destruction, but – in the guise of left wing vs. right wing beliefs – it continues to polarise people to this day, and is the fundamental fault-line in today's political arena, both in the US and elsewhere.

Now I am in no way decrying or nullifying these people's beliefs or their right to them. What I am saying is that in standing up for their beliefs, many (by no means all!) are becoming increasingly intolerant of the fact that others might hold a different view. Often they completely forget the words

---

[35] Gospel of St Matthew 22:37-39 King James version

attributed to Voltaire[36] –"I disagree strongly with every word you say, but I will defend to the death your right to say it!" – and that their stance is increasingly predicated on a specific issue rather than an understanding of the bigger picture. In other words they are caught up with the policy rather than the principle.

So it goes without saying that the way to redress this is to go back to principles, which is precisely what I propose to do now. I will very briefly describe a number of key principles from which I believe we have strayed too far, the restoration of which, and adherence to, would go a long way towards restoring basic democracy and our longer-term economic well-being, thereby enabling us to build the foundations of a better future.

PRINCIPLE ONE: RESPECT FOR OUR FELLOW MAN

Liberty, Equality and Fraternity, as espoused by the original founders of democracy, have been a pretty good foundation. They formed what could perhaps be described as the very first slogan. As such, they provided a very good rallying cry for the early democratic movement and we owe it a huge debt. As we have seen, however, notwithstanding its power, democracy itself has been too easily subverted and a new stance is needed. While it may not be necessary to reinvent the wheel, the slogan is perhaps in need of a revamp to give it greater credibility or, at very least, a re-launch.

"Respect for our fellow man," may encapsulate all the elements, but it does not have the same sizzle, so it may be a good idea to stick to something which stays close to the old form and keeps these elements at its heart.

Though it doesn't roll off the tongue quite so easily, I would propose replacing "equality" with "equitability." After all, we all know that equality is an unrealistic goal. Even if "everyone is equal in the sight of God" we all know that circumstances dictate that people are not equal in circumstances

---

[36] But in fact written by his biographer, Evelyn Beatrice Hall

or in talent or in the opportunities they get in life. There can only be one gold medal winner (other than in a dead-heat!) and we cannot all be the President of the United States or the Prime Minister of Britain. As a rule people can accept this and do not mind other people being "more equal" than them. The difference is only tolerable, however, if people are treated equitably. For equitability implies a combination of equality and fairness and thus is far more reasonable and realistic. While "life is not fair" because of people's innate differences, those people still deserve to be treated equitably and resent any situation in which they are not.

So let's go for a new slogan of "Freedom, Fraternity and Equitability!" as the basis of a new modern democracy and lets ensure that we build these elements into everything we do. Then we will enable that better future we were envisioning!

PRINCIPLE TWO: BALANCE

Remember the theory about Society's 40 year pendulum – swinging from "me" to "we"? Notwithstanding Thomas Mann's stance that this is the inevitable consequence of the fact that freedom and equality are mutually exclusive, perhaps this can be counted as a clearer definition of exactly what freedom entails.

To me freedom is simply the ability to lead my life according to my own beliefs without interference from anyone else, as long as in exercising that freedom I do not infringe the individual or collective rights of my fellow man. Thus freedom is a right and an obligation and both need to be in balance at all times. The only criteria for judging actions should be whether or not they impinge on another's rights.

PRINCIPLE THREE: SELF-FULFILMENT

The principle of equitability is a building block for everybody to lead a life in which they are able to optimise their own talents and fulfil their potential, "to be the best they can be."

This is based on the innate desire to "make a difference" and the three intrinsic motivators, most clearly delineated in Daniel Pink's book *Drive*, which power people's actions, represented by the mnemonic, AMP:

- Autonomy
- Mastery
- Purpose

PRINCIPLE FOUR: EMPLOYEES ARE ALSO INVESTORS

Something that is widely overlooked is that employees are also investors. They might not invest money but they invest something of arguably greater value – their lives.

Given the fact that we all have only one life and that we spend a large proportion of our waking time at work, it seems only right that the time we do spend there should also be recognised as an investment. You will see the implications of this later.

PRINCIPLE FIVE: THERE IS ONLY ONE TAX PAYER

Ultimately all tax is paid by the citizens.

This is something that has been made manifestly clear in the response to the debt crisis in the various European countries. It is the citizens who (arguably) had to bail out the banks and then subsequently bail out the government. Thus all tax policies should be streamlined to think about the ultimate burden to the individual taxpayer.

PRINCIPLE SIX: THERE SHOULD BE A SINGLE FLAT TAX RATE.

The principle of progressive (I call them regressive) tax rates is inherently undemocratic. It runs counter to both the elements of equality and equitability. It lies at the root of all tax avoidance and is a primary factor in many of the issues that have brought us into the current predicament.

PRINCIPLE SEVEN: SIMPLIFY TAX AND ELIMINATE THE CONCEPT OF TAX AVOIDANCE

With the introduction of a flat rate tax it should be possible to streamline and simplify tax legislation significantly. This should also be taken as an opportunity to remove the concept of tax avoidance from the lexicon.

PRINCIPLE EIGHT: BOTTOM-UP DEMOCRACY

If you go back to our original Lincoln definition of democracy as; "government of the people, by the people, for the people" then it is imperative that the people are more involved and have a clearer understanding of what that entails. Thus, in order to protect, maintain and sustain democracy it is essential that:

- People are more involved, and
- Closer to the democratic processes.

To ensure this requires less top-down and more bottom-up government. This can be delivered in accordance with ideas I first proposed in *A Feeling of Worth* and I shall revisit and expand on those ideas.

Right, now let's move on and see how these principles can be put into practice.

BUILDING ON PRINCIPLES

PART THREE
REFORMING SOLUTIONS

CHAPTER ELEVEN
A NEW ACCOUNTING REGIMEN

> "The person who takes a job in order to live –
> that is to say, for the money – has turned himself
> into a slave."
>
> **JOSEPH CAMPBELL**

By definition any organisation comprises a number of people. While numbers vary dramatically no organisation can fulfil its purpose without people. Yet, notwithstanding this, our accounting systems fail signally to recognise the vital part that people play, and effectively regards them as slaves. Yes, we increasingly talk about people as assets, but we do not account for them as assets. In fact we continue to follow the conventions of history and account for them as costs. This is a problem because considering people as assets but treating them as costs creates a dichotomy that causes confusion and breeds contempt and conflict. After all, how can you feel like an asset if you are not treated as an asset? This is significant because behaviours govern perception and hence people's reaction.

We all know that appreciation is one of the greatest extrinsic motivators there is. Appreciation is the obverse of being valued. Being appreciated imparts a sense that you or your actions or both are valued. It engages you and makes you want to do more and better. So if you are running an organisation or heading up a team and you do not value your people they will not be as engaged as they might be and your organisation will never achieve all that it could.

For that reason I passionately believe that there is a need to take the statement that people are assets more literally and account for them as such. This is effectively a way of embedding appreciation into the organisational DNA, in a manner that is equitable and consistent. Of course it is not a new idea and many have made the case over the years, although until now no-one has found an acceptable way to do so. I myself made a strong case for it, and revealed my formula for doing this in *Lean Organisations Need FAT People* and so there is little point in repeating what I said there. Nevertheless, the concept is key to much of what follows and an integral, essential element of the solutions I am proposing. I therefore feel it is both unavoidable and imperative that I take some time here to briefly explain my method for accounting for people as assets and why this is so important.

THE 3 STEP MODEL FOR ACCOUNTING FOR PEOPLE AS ASSETS

Step 1: Accounting for People as Assets

The model begins with the valuation of people as assets. This enables you to:

- Consistently value all your employees individually.
- Aggregate those values to derive a "Human Assets" figure that can be included in a notional balance sheet, along with all your other assets.

Naturally value changes over time. By identifying each and every factor that causes value to change, however, you can record, track and account for these variables, giving you a set of clear rules that enable you to recognise, record and report on values over time. These rules guarantee the consistency of the "formula" and ensure that it is constant, consistent and cannot be manipulated. As long as that is the case, and it is uniformly and universally applied, it actually doesn't matter what the value is and it should not be a barrier to winning employees over to the concept.

Step 2: Non-equity Ownership

Accounting for people as assets in this way opens up a unique possibility for creating non-equity ownership.

Creating Human Assets puts a new class of asset on the balance sheet, but this still has to balance. So there must be some corresponding liability. By keeping things simple, however, and using a simple contra journal entry, you can create an account called "Human Capital." Under normal accounting convention this would be a reserve account on the balance sheet, but, if instead of treating it as a conventional reserve account you were to include it under Owners' Equity, you create the capability to make each employee an "owner" with a stake in the business equal to their asset value.

The beauty of adopting this approach is that it offers an entirely new employee-ownership model whereby:

- You link ownership automatically with employment.
- You make all your employees co-owners of the business.
- There is no equity involved so there are none of the valuation and administration issues that are usually involved with equity schemes.
- There is no cost to either your organisation or your employees.
- Because the ownership is inextricably linked to employment, it would normally automatically end with employment.
- There is nothing in this concept that necessitates any change in the employment contract or existing employment practices.
- There is no dilution in the holding of existing equity shareholders.
- You now have employees who, because they own the business, will now act accordingly. This helps to build greater teamwork because it creates shared values that mean your business literally becomes their business and enables you to develop greater line of sight and organisational integrity.

Step 3: The Rewards of Ownership

The third step in the model deals with the rewards of ownership. Now, because you have:

- Made all your employees owners; and
- Your system of ownership is consistent, equitable and inviolable;

you can contemplate the introduction of a new reward scheme, which is exclusively tied-in with organisational performance.

This entails the concept of the "two-tier dividend." Basically this is a gain-sharing system that takes the idea of the traditional dividend payable to shareholders and applies it to employee-owners as well. So now instead of just paying a dividend to shareholders, you declare a single dividend which you pay in two tranches: as a "capital dividend" (to the equity owners) and as a "labour dividend" to the employee owners.

Perhaps this is better explained by giving an example. Let's say that that you have an after tax profit of £1 million and decide to declare a dividend of ten pence. Normally this would mean that the shareholders would get ten pence for every share they own. With this new employee ownership model, the shareholders will still get ten pence for every share they hold, but in addition every employee will also get a ten pence dividend based on their current human asset value.

Now your immediate response to this may be to say that this will:

- Involve a much larger share of your organisation's profits being distributed; and/or
- Reduce the size of the dividend the shareholders would otherwise have got.

That would not, however, be the case because the 'labour dividend' replaces your existing incentive scheme. In other words, it replaces the amount that you would have paid in bonuses and thus makes it entirely cost neutral for your organisation. Of course it would be an additional cost if you don't currently have any kind of incentive or performance related pay scheme, but there are not many such organisations around today. Bonuses have even become endemic in public services.

Even if you don't have such schemes the greater engagement and inevitably improved overall performance that results will generate returns that will make the cost worthwhile and barely noticeable.

A SOLID FOUNDATION

Perhaps you remain sceptical and are thinking to yourself, "That's all very well, but what's the point. It seems to be a lot of extra work for no additional benefit!" So let's start to look at that challenge by examining how this model fits in with principles we were looking at earlier.

Firstly, the valuation and recording of people as assets certainly gives them more respect and thereby implicitly complies with the principle of freedom, fraternity and equitability far more than any existing system. This works, at the very least, by creating what you might even go so far as to call a "framework for fraternity" through a sense of not just being valued, but also of belonging to the organisation. Of course that is very strongly reinforced by the ownership, which also – because of its universality – creates a real sense of "we are all in this together" and thus a strong sense of shared values and common purpose. This is further reinforced by the fact that it lays a platform for greater autonomy, mastery and purpose, increasing the individual's intrinsic motivation, while simultaneously linking it inextricably to the organisation's performance and so creating an on-going balance between the "me" of the individual and the "we" of the organisation.

All this is in turn cemented by the equitability of the reward sharing, for although employees do not share the rewards equally, they do all share them equitability, by virtue of the fact that the dividend is paid at a uniform, universal rate. The only way that any employee can increase their "labour dividend" is to increase their asset value, and that has to be done in accordance with transparent, rigid and equitable rules that cannot be manipulated.

Added to this is the recognition of the employee's life-investment in their work which will reshape attitudes and consequent behaviours.

With such a firm grounding in solid principles, the organisational performance is likely to be considerably better than it would otherwise have been.

- As a result of giving employees the true benefits of ownership, they will see the rewards of their labours and be more business-like in their work. The benefits of ownership are widely acknowledged – indeed historians attribute the great difference in the development of North America compared to South America to the ideal of land ownership. Both continents were colonised at the same time, and yet the pace of economic development in the North exceed that of the South by a considerable margin. This principle has also been applied in business and there is copious evidence that employee-owned companies considerably outperform similar companies with no employee ownership. As a result of being owners, employees will feel they "have more skin in the game" and thus be more enthused, energetic and engaged, so the profits are likely to be that much greater. (Engaged employees are said to improve returns by anything from 20% to 80% and even more.)
- The equitability of the asset valuation process and the concomitant labour dividend means you will get far less – even none – of the dissatisfaction, disgruntlement and disengagement that is so often associated with traditional incentive schemes, and the cause of so many industrial disputes.
- You will be less likely to have problems with underperformance because peer pressure will come into force and ensure that slackers and skivers are sorted out or

else leave the organisation. Put another way that means that there is less of an onus on managers to drive people's performance. Furthermore you will have an in-built mechanism for optimising your employee numbers as too-many employees will reduce the size and share of the pot available for distribution.
- In fact, building on that, there will less need for measuring and monitoring performance altogether, as performance will be self-policed and rectified without management input – which is in any case perceived as interference and thus undermines autonomy! (All this has been proven over many years by Ricardo Semler at Semco and is detailed in his book, *Maverick*.[37])

You just need to remember that in order to reap all these benefits you need to combine all three steps of the model, because together they create an integrated solution that creates a virtuous cycle. Leave out any one step – there is nothing that compels you to implement all three – and you will significantly reduce your potential benefits. That is the only time when you might find the additional benefit is not worth the effort.

AN ASIDE

If you are struggling to see the justification for making employees owners, or are trapped in the conventional wisdom justification of dividends being the reward for shareholders for the risk of investing their capital, I would remind you about the investment employees make. It might not be money, but it is in fact something even more valuable. They are investing an (often significant) part of their lives in the time they spend at work.

When you look at the human contribution to the organisation in that light, then it seems only right that they should also share in the rewards. In fact, in light of the short-term

---

[37] 'Maverick' by Ricardo Semler © Tableturn Inc 1993 Published by Random House. Amazingly the Semco model is taught as a case study at leading business schools around the world and yet no-one has emulated his example. Sometimes conventional wisdom is considerably more solid, sacred and sacrosanct than we would ever believe.

thinking so manifest in the problems we have been examining, employees arguably have a greater vested interest in the long-term sustainability of the organisation than the financial investors. Consequently, it is not only economic justice, but sound economic sense.

That is why I included this in my list of principles.

APPLYING THE EMPLOYEE OWNERSHIP MODEL IN NON-PROFIT ORGANISATIONS

Perhaps you can see and recognise all these benefits but are still sceptical and thinking to yourself, "That's all very well, for regular "for-profit" organisations, but I work in the public sector or for a non-profit organisation. We don't have share-holders or make a profit, so none of this applies in our organisation."

That's a fair challenge, but let me turn your doubts right back on you and ask you a couple of questions.

1. Why don't you think it could be applied in your kind of organisation? For starters you don't have shareholders so instead of having a two-tier dividend split between shareholders and employees you can have a single labour dividend that you pay to your employees. I would say that makes it easier for you, as there is one major barrier that you won't have to address that "for-profit" companies do!
2. Do you currently have a performance related pay or incentive remuneration scheme in place? If you do, then there is absolutely no reason why you couldn't adopt this model; and if you don't then there is even more reason to adopt this model.

So, having knocked that on head, let's take a look and see how you could introduce it.

The primary – in fact the only – requirement for introducing a labour dividend is a consistent basis for determining the pool of funds from which it is to be calculated. Now even if you don't have profits you still have something called 'net income' representing the difference between your organisational income and your expenses. And, if you are running your organisation effectively and efficiently, you should still be trying to maximise your revenue and minimise your costs. By definition, therefore, you should be trying to optimise your net income. So consequently the change in your net income, from one year to the next, is indicative of your performance. Thus this delta should be the first place you look for determining what you can afford to distribute in the way of dividends – even if the charitable nature of your organisation and the need to maximise the good you are doing for your cause means spending virtually all your income. Even then you need to build up reserves for future contingencies, and so you should still have some surplus to enable this. Don't forget, this is not additional expenditure that you are being expected to incur. It is simply an offset of money that you may already being paying out as performance-related pay and bonuses.

That is just my suggestion. I remain open to other ideas if you have them, as long as they adhere to the fundamental principles, at which we have been looking.

TALKING SURPLUSES

There is an additional point about net income that I need to make here. Remember in Chapter Three I made the point that distinguishing between the different sectors and the way they account is, in many ways, a fallacious exercise. My reasoning is that public sector organisations and charities have an even greater obligation to manage resources more prudently and frugally than "for-profit" businesses.

Well, hopefully you can get a clearer sense of this now. The fact is that, technically, there is no fundamental difference between net income and profit. From an accounting perspective they are both what remains after deducting expenses from income or revenue. Consequently, if you agree with the principle that "not-for-profit" organisations have a greater moral obligation to manage their resources frugally you will understand the point, and thus be willing to concede the point that all organisations should focus some attention on the bottom line – the surplus or deficit that arises from that equation, and perhaps adopt the term "surplus" as a new standard regardless.

(We will return to this point again later and perhaps I will be better able to help you understand why it is so important.)

ADVANTAGES OF THIS MODEL OF EMPLOYEE-OWNERSHIP OVER TRADITIONAL SHARE SCHEMES

If you are more conversant with traditional equity based share schemes you may, at the back of your mind, still be asking yourself why it would be worthwhile to adopt this model rather than a more traditional equity type scheme. After all these are increasingly popular, and have been found to be one of the best ways of enhancing employee engagement.

Notwithstanding this there are still a number of handicaps with employee share ownership schemes. These include:

- When the shares are listed on the stock exchange:
    - The insignificant holdings made available, which don't really give the employee any real sense of ownership or control.
    - The formalities and need to comply with strict regulatory guidelines.
- When the shares are not listed:
    - The difficulty in valuing shares.
    - The difficulty in liquidating the shares when there is a need.
- Generally such schemes favour the upper echelons of the company and exacerbate the sense that they are not really for everyone but just a sop to the rest.
- Related to the last point, is the fact that for lower paid employees "cash is king" because they need more to meet their everyday living expenses. This means that they tend to sell their shares as soon as they can and thus negate the so-called benefits of the scheme.

This employee-ownership model therefore better delivers the intended benefits of share ownership because:

- As we have seen, it does not have to be limited to only private sector, equity companies i.e. you could introduce it into the public sector, NGO's, social enterprises and charities.
- Every employee is – and remains – an owner as long as they remain employed.
- The distribution of ownership is equitable and tends to remain equitable (because of the consistency and inviolability of your human asset valuation rules.)
- There is no equity and, therefore, no trading of one's stake.

Basically with this model the focus remains 100% on the business, and does not get subverted by concerns about the share price, which can be affected by factors outside the company's and the employees' control.

A COMPLETELY DIFFERENT PERSPECTIVE

You will, I am sure, agree that these are pretty significant benefits. They are, not however, all that this model offers. As you would perhaps expect, because it takes such a different approach to business, it also has profound implications for the way in which we look at a business. I would like to give an example to illustrate this now, and in order to do I would like to take you back to Chapter Five when, talking about policy perversion, I gave an example to explain why "sequestration is a silly way to do business."[38]

---

[38] Please remember that the "Sequestration" referred to here is simply a US term to describe the forced budget cutting as a result of the fact that the US has reached its constitutional borrowing limit and the impasse in negotiations between the parties. It does not have the normal meaning of the legal seizure of property and has no other direct relevance to the subject. As far as I know "sequestration" does not apply anywhere other than the US, which is the only country to have a constitutional borrowing constraint – although this was something I argued for in "A Feeling of Worth."

This illustrates beautifully some of the key conventional business thinking that dictates how business is administered and managed. I have italicised these in the text box below.

Sequestration Is a Silly Way to Do Business

Imagine you had a small business that employed ten people. Two were brilliant workers who added tremendous value to your company and increased its profitability. *Two of your employees were slackers who seriously underperformed in their duties. The rest were average workers.*

Now let's say *the bad economy was affecting your business and forced you to make a 20% cut in your payroll.* Which of these two scenarios would be smarter?

1. Fire the two underperforming employees, eliminating 20% of your workforce; or

2. Slash 20% of all 10 employees' salary on an equal basis.

A wise business owner would never pick #2 and punish his star employees in order to be "fair" to the slackers. That's plain silly.

But that's what a government sequester is all about: Every department pays equally. Across-the board cuts without taking into consideration the value of the program.

---

1. There is an assumption that some of your workers are simply slackers and that, much as you would like to, there is nothing you can do about it.
2. There is the standard response to a bad economy; namely that it inevitably means that you have to cut your payroll costs.
3. There is a token admission that there is an alternative to redundancy, but that it is one which "a wise business owner" would never take.
4. There is a misconception that it is "unfair" and "silly" to "punish star employees."

Hopefully by simply highlighting them in this way you can see how much our thinking is governed by conventional wisdom, for each one of these attitudes is open to challenge, even though they so seldom are.

1. The fact that the business is carrying "slackers" is indicative of poor management. No good manager should tolerate slackers and the fact that he does is:
    a) An indictment of him or her as a manager;
    b) An indication that optimum performance is only a token objective;
    c) Evidence of the fact that "fairness" only comes into the equation when times are bad and other than that the general feelings of employees count for nothing, even if they are "stars."
2. A properly managed business should be able to handle the good times and bad times with almost equal aplomb.
3. A "wise business owner" would never get rid of key assets due to bad economic conditions or else would only do so under extreme circumstances, so why then should he get rid of his human assets. Studies show that getting rid of people always has a long term negative effect on the business, and that it takes longer to recover than if it had not laid people off.
4. Isn't it "unfair" to deprive any employee of their livelihood – especially when every redundancy is said to impact upon at least 4 people?

All that's before you even start looking at what this model will achieve. Let's take a look, however, at what this model does in regard to these points.

1. Because it starts from the principle that the organisation is ultimately a single team, it invokes a common purpose and the kind of distributed leadership and peer pressure that would not tolerate "slack" workers. They would be forced to "shape up

or ship out" by their colleagues, let alone their managers.
2. The employees as a single team would also mean:
   a) The business would be more likely to be in better position to face up to and see out the bad times and "take the strain."
   b) As a result of the fact that people are seen to be assets, far more consideration will be given to their treatment and there would be less inclination to simply "cut costs." You would have people all working together to try to find solutions and come up with new ways to take the business forward.
3. If there was no alternative than to reduce staff costs and/or let people go, the people themselves could be involved in deciding the best way to do this, rather than having a solution arbitrarily imposed upon them.
4. The employees as a caring, sharing team would consider it far fairer if they were involved in any such decision process, and accept the decision with more equanimity.

MACRO-ECONOMIC BENEFITS

These benefits we have been looking at so far are all at the organisational or micro-level. However, they have a massive macro-economic effect too. Remember in Chapter Two we saw how the income gap was growing and the wealth gap was growing as a result. Well, this model addresses the root cause of that problem, too. The equitability of the new reward system and the labour dividend means that you will no longer get the extremely high earners getting 100% plus bonuses on their enormous base salaries while the lower level employees get a 5-10% bonus on their comparatively small bases. Everyone will now get a labour dividend, at the same rate, paid in accordance with their asset value. This will make society as a whole more democratic, not only in accordance with the traditional concepts of liberty, equality and fraternity, but – hopefully – but also by eliminating what I call the "human economic waste" of the underutilised intelligence and capabilities of people within an organisation. They will also help to reduce the tensions that, as we have seen, are putting both democracy and the whole economic system under stress, and ultimately pose a threat to their continued existence.

In addition this employee-ownership model also offers further macro-economic benefits by creating a unique opportunity for changing the tax system, as you will see in the next chapter.

A NEW ACCOUNTING REGIMEN

CHAPTER TWELVE
A NEW TAX REGIMEN

> "It is your tax which pays for public spending. The government have no money of their own. There is only the taxpayers' money."
>
> **MARGARET THATCHER**

Governments receive the bulk of their revenue through taxes. Good government, therefore, depends on having reliable tax systems for both raising and collecting those taxes. This in turn means that taxpayers need to know for what taxes they are liable and to have the capability to plan, prepare for and pay the taxes they owe. This requires transparency and openness.

Unfortunately, this is increasingly not the case. Our tax systems are becoming ever more complex and currently failing us so badly that they are in urgent need of re-engineering. Earlier you saw that there are at least three key reasons why tax revenues are declining:

- Industrial scale tax avoidance and the widening wealth gap it exacerbates;
- Reduced corporate taxes;
- The elimination of jobs through off-shoring.

Each of these is indicative of systemic failings and these have to be addressed. And that does not even include the fact that the more complex are the tax structures, the greater the cost of collection, which further reduces the amount the Government has to spend.

ELIMINATING TAX AVOIDANCE

Tax avoidance on the scale we saw exemplified by Barclays poses a very real threat to the long-term sustainability of society as we know it. It is, therefore, something that needs to be redressed as a matter of urgency, yet government efforts to do so seem to lack bite, and a cynic could easily argue they are more for show than effect; a sop to those who can vote but otherwise lack economic power.

After all the problem could be easily addressed because tax avoidance can be attributed to three key, inter-linked factors:

- Progressive tax rates and the higher rates of marginal tax;
- The complexity of tax legislation which makes it possible; and
- The legitimacy of efforts to minimise tax.

Progressive tax rates are the direct consequence of social engineering. The concept is underpinned by the well-intentioned (and legitimate) belief that the more fortunate in society need to help the less fortunate. The conventional wisdom has interpreted fortunate to mean more affluent and taxes have, therefore, become the legitimate means to "re-distribute wealth" with that being an explicit commitment of tax regulation.

Unfortunately it is inherently undemocratic and that is the root of the problem.

How can you espouse the cause of democracy with the concept of all men being equal if you have a tax system that is undemocratic to the core? Let's look at a simple, hypothetical example to see what this means in practice.

X has a taxable income of $20,000 and pays tax at 10%

Y has a taxable income of $1 million and pays tax at 45%

Under current regulations that means X pays tax of $1,000, after deducting their $10,000 tax free amount. By contrast with the same $10,000 tax free amount (and, for ease of calculation, ignoring the fact that 45% is the marginal tax rate) Y would pay income tax of $445,500.

On the other hand if Y was taxed on the same basis as X at 10% they would "only" pay $99,000.

Even at this lower rate Y would still pay virtually ten times what X pays, which is entirely equitable in view of the fact that they earn ten times as much.

Now look at it from another perspective. The difference between the rate Y actually pays ($445,500) and the rate they would pay at the more equitable 10% ($99,000) is $346,500: a pretty good incentive for Y to see what they could do to avoid paying the full amount, wouldn't you say?

And that inequitability is the fundamental cause of the problem, and is further compounded by the recognition of its likelihood and the legal allowances that entitles Y to do all they can to legitimately reduce their tax bill. This increases the complexity of tax legislation and means there is a never-ending game, whereby taxpayers do all they can to find loopholes to avoid tax and governments follow up with new legislation to close those loopholes.

As a result you:

- Get a whole industry developing around tax avoidance à-la our Barclays example;
- An inordinate amount of expected revenue being "lost";
- Some of the best brains in society being put to what is ultimately a not very productive use.

(And that's ignoring the fundamental economic question of whether Y can use that $346,000 more efficiently and effectively than government, which is notorious for its waste. This opportunity cost issue creates the potential for one of those never-ending philosophical debates, but in a world that is looking more consciously, more conscientiously and more consistently for greater sustainability and the best use of resources to safeguard that, perhaps it is not irrelevant.)

Be that as it may, all these tax avoidance issues could be easily avoided by introducing a single rate tax system, with severe consequences for anyone who does not pay the full taxes they ought to. This would:

- Be more equitable and thus more democratic;

- Dramatically simplify tax legislation;
- Eliminate the need for a tax industry;
- Most likely be more economically efficient;
- Put an end to the redistribution of wealth convention, which self-evidently is not working as evidenced by the fact that the wealth-gap is widening rather than narrowing;
- Reduce the cost of collecting tax.

There is, however, still one aspect of tax avoidance that we have not considered in all this – corporate tax avoidance. There is nothing to suggest that tax avoidance is a purely personal phenomenon. Consequently we also need to consider this. Here too there is a very simple – albeit considerable more radical – remedy: eliminate corporation tax.

I bet that has got you throwing up your hands in horror, but let's have a look at the subject in greater depth and explore just how feasible it could be, and why it may actually be a solution to many of the issues we have been looking at, and something that could really help us enable that better future, to which we aspire. We should take Margaret Thatcher's, statement "Our aim is to make tax collection a declining industry" and change it to "Our aim is to kill tax avoidance as an industry."

ELIMINATING CORPORATION TAX

Of course if you have an already over-burdened taxpayer, logically it would appear sensible to expect businesses to pay a greater share, but businesses are themselves a victim of a depressed economy, and, if you are looking to stimulate growth and greater prosperity, looking to businesses to pay more tax also does not make sound economic sense. Even so, the idea of eliminating corporation tax may seem a little extreme, but if you think about it for a moment you will see that there are a number of good reasons why business tax does not actually make sound economic sense.

Firstly, profit is easily manipulated and thus an artificial and perhaps economically unsound basis for assessing tax. (Believe me – I am an accountant and I know!) Why? Because if you have two identical companies operating with precisely the same resources the less efficient will make smaller profits and therefore pay less tax. This effectively means that the taxpayer is effectively subsidising the less efficient. Surely that is not the basis on which you want to run a sound economy! Or, for that matter, one that is environmentally aware and optimising the use of scarce resources effectively.

It comes back to that divide between commerce and economics: profit is a commercial concept and not an economic one. Remember too Newton's law that for every action there is an equal and opposite reaction, which means that there is no scientific basis for it. There may be no reasonable, viable alternative to profit or an equivalent for commercial purposes, but there is no need to use profit as a basis for assessing tax.

Secondly, it completely destroys the questionable-but-never-questioned premise that tax planning should be part of management. In a Harvard Business Review article[39] calling for a better tax system, Professor Mihir Desai points out that; "avoidance behaviours are pervasive in good management." This is apart from the fact the need for a corporation to make good profits means that prices may well be higher than they would be if it was not paying tax at all. This means that the man in the street is effectively paying a higher price than he might otherwise pay. Thus once again it is the average citizen who effectively ends up paying the tax.

Furthermore, Professor Desai argues that higher corporate tax rates result in businesses becoming uncompetitive and losing out to foreign competition.

Perhaps a good example of this is the bond sale by Apple. Here, taking advantage of the record low interest rates Apple, in the biggest ever non-banking bond sale, went to the market to raise $17.5 billion in order to "fund its plan for extra pay-

---

[39] "A Better Way to Tax US Businesses" by Mihir A. Desai, Mizuho Finance Group Professor at Harvard Business School. Harvard Business Review 1 July 2012

outs to shareholders",[40] in accordance with its plan to buy back $60 billion in shares from its shareholders and increase the dividend. Now you might not think that there is anything wrong with this, but I can think of several reasons why this is, at best, a dubious decision and morally questionable:[41]

- It simply seems daft to pay out money that you don't have to, and even more daft to borrow in order to do so, no matter how low the interest rates.
- If you agree it is daft to borrow money on this scale, you must agree it is absolutely insane to do so when your balance sheet shows cash reserves of $145 billion! This is borrowing money that will yield no (obvious) return.
- If the company continues to decline as the current fall in profits seem to suggest, the share buy-back may disadvantage the remaining shareholders (unless, of course, the buy-back is spread equitably across the entire shareholder base.)
- The rationale for Apple not utilising its own money for this is apparently because repatriating it will cost too much in tax. So where then is the benefit to the national economy of off-shoring?
- It illustrates the extent to which management thinking is distorted by tax considerations and underscores the divide between economic and commercial thinking. (And once again the biggest winners are likely to be the banks and financial institutions handling the whole bond issue, for they will get paid regardless of how successful the issue turns out to be.)

All this supports my earlier point that the cost of the lost revenue and profits moving offshore is once again borne by the citizens of the country losing the jobs, and is ultimately detrimental to the long-term sustainability of the national econ-

---

[40] BBC News report 1 May 2013 http://www.bbc.co.uk/news/business-22361840
[41] Apple already has prior in this regard apparently having avoided $74 billion tax between 2009-2012 – a fact they do not deny. Source. "Leaders Eat Last" Simon Sinek © 2104 Penguin

omy of the country in which the business is domiciled. This, however, underscores a further issue: namely that our current tax systems are grounded in the post-war industrial era and are no longer appropriate for a globally competitive world. The fact is that global competition increasingly means that countries are competing against one another and to perhaps an even greater extent than businesses, which are increasingly international in the outlook and relatively free to relocate their headquarters anywhere in the world it is expedient to do so. The fear that the financial sector will relocate from London is a major factor in the UK government's unwillingness to do more to introduce measures to check the powers of bankers in the wake of the financial crisis.

So there you have three very good reasons why business taxes do not make sound economic sense.

Furthermore, there may be grounds for challenging the logic of the assumption that by taxing profits before any distribution to owners you are taking away any personal pain.

The stakeholders of an organisation are a collective of people and all these people are distinct, different and have a varying degree of involvement with the organisation. For instance a financial stakeholder may have a very remote link to the organisation, as a lender or owner, particularly if – as is often the case with large public corporations – ownership is held through an intermediary in the form of a hedge fund or pension fund. Then they might not even be aware of their connection. In such circumstances the risk associated with their stake may be insignificant. In any event, in most cases it is unlikely to be their entire financial wellbeing that is at stake. For employees, however, it may well be different. Even ignoring my earlier point that they are actually "investing" their lives in their work, they may have their entire livelihood at stake, and thus their well-being and that of their family and dependents.

For this reason at least the traditional viewpoint that shareholders have the biggest stake in the organisation and its long-term success needs to be re-evaluated and with it the basis of levying taxes on the organisation. The model of employee ownership described in the last chapter is an ideal way of recognising and accommodating this.

THE ALTERNATIVE TO CORPORATION TAX

Of course business taxes represent a significant proportion of a government's revenue. Consequently it is extremely difficult to make the case to dispense with such taxes. Governments have obligations to meet on behalf of their citizens and the loss of a significant proportion of their revenue would obviously jeopardise that capability. So is there an alternative to businesses paying tax? There is, but it needs to be thought through very carefully.

In all likelihood merely eliminating business taxes would result in greater profits with a greater share being paid in executive bonuses. This would exacerbate the national problem for two reasons.

- Firstly it would increase the wealth gap between the rich and the poor. This is already a major problem and exacerbating it would only cause greater dissatisfaction, without achieving any of the objectives you intended by dispensing with business taxes in the first place.
- Secondly, and perhaps more significantly, the recipients of this additional income are the same people who have become adept at tax avoidance. The proportion of their total income paid in taxes is already considerably lower than that paid by ordinary citizens. This would further reduce government's revenue and exacerbate the problem of the widening earnings gap. Tax avoidance is increasingly becoming a headline issue and this would be a recipe for wider dissatisfaction and possible unrest. The Occupy movements already provide evidence that ordinary people are mistrustful of the current environment and getting restive and this would do nothing to reassure them and could inflame them further.

Consequently any solution would have to ensure that it overcomes these two potential problems. Once again this boils down to recognising that it is the individual citizen who is playing the role of Atlas and carrying the economy on their shoulders. This requires a two-pronged solution and you have already seen both prongs:

1. Our new model of employee ownership; and
2. A single flat tax rate.

Neither will reap their full reward without the other.

Employee ownership, with employees receiving a greater reward for their efforts, would ensure a wider distribution of the rewards of business to all who contribute to the organisation (whether for profit or not-for-profit), and thus encourage a more productive work-force that would be more likely to stimulate the national economic performance. From a tax perspective, however, it would also mean there was a more consistent platform from which the government might levy taxes.

In order to do this and maximise the benefits while ensuring that it receives all the revenue to which it is entitled, the government would self-evidently have to change the tax structures. Yet this need not be a major obstacle and could easily be done by a more equitable, universal, single-rate tax system. As already indicated this offers a viable solution for several reasons.

A lower rate and less avoidance. It creates the opportunity to have a lower rate that is likely to be more appealing to taxpayers paying a higher marginal rate. This will make tax avoidance less of an issue and less tempting, especially if the penalties are strengthened and more stringently enforced, with a stigma being attached to the tax avoider as being someone who is not willing to make their contribution to society. For any government looking for the mandate to implement new initiatives this is also likely to be a vote winner!

Simpler legislation and easier collection. A flat rate eliminates complexity and reduces the amount of legislation required. (The UK Income Tax Act is (apparently) currently more than 11,000 pages!) In addition it will fit with existing payroll deduction procedures and make collection straightforward with a larger collection pool. It will eliminate the secondary industry that has grown up around avoiding tax and thus put some of the smarter minds to more productive use for the greater good of society as a whole.

Reduced offshoring. This model effectively makes all tax a payroll tax, and means collection will occur where the work is carried out. This may possibly reduce off-shoring on its own, but would further inhibit the transfer of profits due to the self-interest of the employee owners and their reluctance to forego a share of their labour dividends and/or the capital for developing the business further. It will means that companies like Amazon, Google and Starbucks will all contribute far more to the revenue system than they are at present; even if it is indirectly through their payroll deductions

Narrow the wage gap. As already indicated this will go a considerable way towards closing the ever widening pay gap. People will still be able to earn more both through this new reward-sharing model and the additional motivation for self-improvement that this will stimulate, but this will be aligned to their value and always remain equitable relative to that of their colleagues and fellow citizens. This will go a considerable way towards avoiding the jealousy, disputes and industrial conflicts that have pervaded history for the past two-hundred and fifty years, as well as reduce the likelihood of insurrection and revolution that has been starting to manifest itself in the Occupy movements.

The imperatives for change

If those are not imperatives enough to contemplate change, you can also add in the four imperatives that Professor Desai outlined in his article as demanding change.

High rates and a narrow base. This issue was raised specifically to the US where corporate tax rates are now apparently amongst the highest in the world and so reducing US competitiveness. (See what I mean about increasing national competitiveness? This point was further underscored in the 2013 UK budget when the Chancellor of the Exchequer announced reduced corporate tax rates that made "Britain the best country in the world to do business!") It remains an issue, however, in any tax system with variable rates when higher rates result in less revenue because the highest income earners are best placed to exploit tax avoidance loopholes. This is something getting increasing press and is a further sign of tough times and declining living standards. It is, however, also sickeningly tedious here in the UK to watch the leaders of the two major political parties continue their Punch and Judy act on the subject, with the opposition decrying the reduction of the highest marginal tax rate from 50% to 45% as "a reward for the wealthy on the backs of the poor who are suffering in these difficult times." Those complaining are the self-same people that had reduced it themselves when in government, acknowledging the futility of excessively high rates and had only increased them again as a political gesture.

This proposal certainly addresses the issue and puts it firmly to bed, once and for all. The complete elimination of Corporation Tax effectively creates a zero rate and you simply cannot go lower than that! Yet it does not simply wipe out a whole tranche of revenue. Rather it creates a viable alternative that offers the direct opposite – a very low rate across the broadest possible base. It would significantly reduce the capital flow out of the country and help ensure local investment and the concomitant maintenance and improvement of the national standard of living.

The rise of non-corporate business income. This apparently refers to the 150% growth of non-corporate income from 20% to 50% of business income since 1986, as the result of legislative restructuring aimed at reducing or avoiding tax. I cannot speak with any authority about this US specific situation, but it seems that this refers to US companies (like Apple) not paying "their fair share" of the corporate tax in the same way that Amazon, Google and Starbucks are not paying it in the UK. It certainly seems that this proposal would remedy that, for it makes organisational structure irrelevant in the context of tax collection and thus eliminates any need for this.

The UK, however, is grappling with the opposite issue. Here there is a mounting attack on people who have left full time employment and created limited companies through which they are billing their work, often at considerably higher rates than they earned previously and with the added benefit of reduced tax liabilities (especially if they get a good tax advisor to guide them through the tax avoidance loopholes that we looked at earlier!) Nevertheless, it does seem ironic that this should be criticised, not least by a right wing coalition government, when it is nothing more than capitalism personified. There can be little doubt that hiring contractors in this way does increase the cost of government procurement, but – assuming there was no tax avoidance (or that loopholes permitting it were closed) – it would be interesting to research how much the net cost to the government would be because critics also forget that these people now also pay VAT and although they are able to deduct their input costs the government exchequers should still benefit considerably from this.

This solution, however, also eliminates this problem, as the amount of tax that would be collected from the individual should be the same, certainly in the longer term, because there is no longer any differentiation between salary and dividend income. (Under this scheme the "labour dividend" would still be income rather than dividend.)

The globalisation of firm activity. This refers to the apparent increase in non-domestic activity as a result of increased foreign investment pursuing greater profits offshore. According to Desai this has resulted in money not being repatriated in order to avoid the effect of the additional taxes after double-taxation relief, due to the aforementioned uncompetitive US corporate tax rates. This solution should help address this problem as well, for the US is apparently unique amongst developed nations in taxing the world-wide income of its corporations.

Globalisation has, however, resulted in a new era of mobility which means that corporations can change their national identities with ease. This is a worry for any government that derives a significant proportion of its income from corporate taxes, as evidenced by the government's fear in face of the threat of the Financial Services industry to move from the UK when threatened with punitive taxes for the mismanagement that led to the 2008 financial crisis. This is a significant threat for a country that has sacrificed its manufacturing base to become one of the world's leading financial centres. A single rate tax and the elimination of corporation tax may not eliminate that threat completely, but it certainly mitigates it.

The decoupling of financial and taxable income. This refers to the fact that there is an increasing gap between reported profits and the base against which tax is paid. There are apparently many reasons for this, including tax policies for such items as depreciation and the growth of investment in such activities that are ultimately non-productive and have a significant opportunity cost. This is not just a US phenomenon, but is also seen in the earlier examples of companies like Amazon and Starbucks paying no tax on their significant UK profits. This proposal eliminates the tax aspects entirely and so provides an ideal solution here, too.

(I cannot help wondering if these concerns support my point about the futility of profit as a measure of economic performance. Whether they do or not, however, the model I am proposing furthers the case for the universal adoption of a generic "surplus" measure, with less emphasis on the concept of "profits".)

POLITICAL RAPPROCHEMENT

One additional point worth making is that this proposition has more going for it than simply endorsing the principle of equality that underpins democracy. While it possibly deserves consideration on those grounds alone, it also offers a healthy fusion of the best of capitalism and socialism and so has the potential to cut through the ideological issues that have caused so much conflict and hardship over the past century or so. It retains all the basic elements of capitalism and the unprecedented success it has achieved in raising living standards, while tempering it with greater worker rights that will moderate its worst excesses and much of what has led us into the economic mess in which we now find ourselves. In fact you could argue that it is the ultimate capitalist model in so far as it makes capitalists out of everyone, but at the same time it does this in a structure that moves beyond the basic worker co-operative model and is thus inherently socialist.

A more modern development in this ideological divide in the UK was the drive for privatisation, spear-headed by Margaret Thatcher and her government. This is a lightning rod that really divides public opinion. Protagonists see her initiative to sell off state institutions and run them among more commercial lines as the catalyst for growth and economic development that powered the economic boom and which was responsible for British prosperity through the turn of the century. Opponents regard it as little more than a ploy to enrich Tory cronies and the already wealthy.

Regardless of the camp into which you fall, the emotions aroused by the subject run deep and it is unlikely that consensus will ever be reached. One consequence of this is that the threat of "being privatised" is one of the greatest fears pervading the public sector today, and drives much of the opposition to Coalition efforts to try to reduce government expenditure. It is simply regarded as the thin edge of the wedge in an attempt to bring about more privatisation. Thus there is a great deal of mistrust, which is particularly strong around the subject of NHS reform, despite what may be the Coalition's biggest mistake: the decision to exclude the NHS from their cost-saving initiatives.

This proposal cuts through that. It embodies everything I mean when I say principles rather than policies should shape behaviour, and I believe that it builds on sound principles that will bring people on opposite sides of the political spectrum together in a true spirit of collaboration. By empowering the people to a greater extent than ever before it achieves one of the great ideals of socialism while at the same time it limits the potential risk of "covert capitalisation" of the type that has led us into the economic mess of "the second great depression." It, therefore, offers the prospect for developing a new platform of greater co-operation that will cut through the old political divides and party political systems and enable new solutions to be devised that will benefit everyone.

THE OTHER SIDE OF THE COIN

You may recall that earlier I suggested that the revenue collection and the expenditure arms of Government should be divided. These ideas will certainly go a long way towards enabling this to become a practical reality. In the same way that the collection will be simpler, more efficient and more cost-effective, expenditure will be too, especially if it is overseen at the local level rather than centrally at the national level.

One of the biggest problems here in the UK, and perhaps more widely throughout Europe, now that we are facing up to the excessive debt described earlier, is the need to cut "benefits" (social welfare payments to the less fortunate in our society.) Like it or not, people are having to face up to the situation that I predicted in *A Feeling of Worth*, namely the fact that government cannot continue to spend money in the way to which they appear to have grown accustomed and as if it grew on trees. Government expenditure reduction programmes, or "austerity measures" as they are widely called, have become a necessity – even if the idea is not accepted by many who have got too used to the earlier largesse.

This is inevitably a rod for Government's back. The problem, however, is exacerbated by two major factors:

- The centralised nature of government; and
- The sheer number and variety of benefits on offer.

The former creates problems precisely because of the inversion that I described earlier and government's remoteness from the recipients of these benefits. You now have a situation where rules and regulations are being decreed from on high but are having to be implemented at the coal-face by people who are genuinely trying to help and who feel strongly that cuts are morally wrong.

Furthermore, because there are so many different benefits, each channel of delivery feels the pressure and squawks. Thus the resentment, resistance and opposition spreads wider than it otherwise might, which all makes the proposed changes easier to oppose, and leaves each minister to fight their own battles against a massed 'army', mobilised by trade unions with the on-going threat of strike action.

Perhaps one of the worst outcomes of all this, however, is the tension it has created between central and local government. In the UK, central government has instructed local governments not to increase their council rates, which, while it makes sense in such difficult economic times, you will have to agree, hardly conforms to the principles of democracy (notwithstanding the Prime Minister's "that's democracy" response to over a third of all local government refusing to do so!) This, I am afraid, simply awakens my cynicism and appears to send the message that it is not central government's responsibility if local government doesn't toe the line, and, therefore, the taxpayers should hold their local governments responsible if their taxes are going up, and not blame the central government.

That is why it is imperative that we nip this in the bud and correct this inversion of democracy. Having taxes allocated at the local level, with the first slice going to local government, will enable money to be allocated to local programmes first and thus do far more to ensure that government is indeed "for the people." It will be a foundation stone for ensuring that problems are addressed at the community level where there is a greater chance of success because the chain of responsibility is not so long and the people responsible can be held more accountable without the finger-pointing that goes on between the different levels of government.

This would be further enhanced by:

- Legislating the proportion of tax revenues that are remitted to central government (a suggestion I first proposed in *A Feeling of Worth*); and
- Ensuring that there is some representation from local government in the national parliament. By this I mean that there should be someone from local government who also sits in at the national legislative body, so that (in good management speak) there is a clearer line-of-sight between the two levels and, therefore, greater co-ordination.

All this would make it considerably easier to address the second issue and streamline the number of 'benefits' available.

STREAMLINING BENEFIT PAYMENTS

The subject of benefits is an emotive one that incites great passion and polarises society. I would, however, like to stay clear of taking any sides on the issue and, as far as possible, stick to working from principles. I believe that benefits are a good example of an area where policy divides – exacerbated by the fact that it is always more difficult to take away something once given than not to give it in the first place – along the way having made things more complicated than they need to have been and caused avoidable conflict.

As you would expect, the principles I am talking about here are those we have been looking at earlier, which underpin democracy. Benefits are possibly the meeting place of Thomas Mann's point that "society and the individual are mutually exclusive." This is because in their objective to make men equal they take away from one individual to give to another. Looking after society's less fortunate inevitably means taking from the more fortunate, and it is only the democratic belief in fraternity that makes this possible. Problems arise, however, when this redistribution is legislated and, that is effectively what our tax laws do: they legislate the redistribution. Unfortunately this creates two root issues:

- It removes any independence from the process; and
- It is not, as you have already seen, always equitable.

These root issues manifest themselves in many different ways, and it is probably not worth spending any time trying to identify them here. Suffice to say that benefits cause resentment if the money is not used in a manner in which the taxpayer approves. Naturally the more different benefits there are, the more susceptible to criticism the process becomes, especially when they can be perceived as unmerited or rewarding the undeserving. (You should never forget that perceptions rather than reality govern thinking when it comes to these matters.) Consequently, streamlining and reducing their number would go a long way towards reducing this risk of resentment.

SOCIAL PAYMENTS

It is important, however, to remember that benefits are not the only disbursements that Government makes to taxpayers. For example it also pays out pensions to citizens who are no longer working. I am not going to try to list all the payments government makes to its citizens, (not least because they will vary from country to country) but I think bringing them all under the administration of local government would present an ideal opportunity to co-ordinate them all, as well as to reduce the current burden and cost of administration. Apart from anything else, aligning them with tax and payroll deduction systems, will simplify the process and make means-testing seamless and virtually transparent. This will allow regressive payments which, although they are as undemocratic as progressive tax rates, are more justifiable – particularly in the current economic climate. Not only is the concept more defensible but it is also more equitable and will reduce the openness of the system to criticism. It thus offers a practical solution to the conundrum described by Mann referred to earlier.

To facilitate this I would recommend having social payments divided into three main categories:

- Life payments: permanent or on-going payments to those that need them e.g. Anybody who is disabled, incompetent or unable to care for themselves.
- Pension payments: on-going payments to senior citizens who have contributed to the National Insurance Fund (or its equivalent) during their working lives.
- Insurance payments: temporary payments to those who have suffered a misfortune that prevents them from carrying out their lives in the same way which they could before and, without which, they would be so much worse off that they would be unable to maintain their standard of living and risk sliding into poverty. e.g. Jobseekers allowances.

I might also add a fourth category of Health Insurance being temporary (and perhaps in some case permanent) payments to cover the costs of poor health to ensure that the person is not placed in financial difficulties as a result of health issues. In the UK this would replace the unsustainable NHS system while still providing a safety net for the less affluent. In the US it would create a safety net that does not appear to exist and prevent people falling into the poverty trap because of medical bills or the less affluent being unable to receive the treatment or care they need. (It seems to me that there is something seriously amiss in the most affluent nation in the world, when people clamour for an (archaic) constitutional right to bear arms but not to be afforded care if they need it.

That cannot be the American dream – especially if people who have previously paid their way and due to circumstances beyond their control are no longer able to carry on as they once did. The democratic element of fraternity has definitely been lost there.)

Clearly there need to be some guiding rules for such payments, but those would need to be defined by others and not by me. The only requirement I would insist upon is that nobody is able to benefit indefinitely at society's expense if they are capable of doing more than they appear willing to do. As I argued in *A Feeling of Worth* I believe that detracts from their sense of self-worth and is ultimately detrimental to both them and the wider community. It all comes back to equitability. People are not equal, but as long as everyone has had a fair chance to make the best of themselves then they have to be responsible and held accountable for their own circumstances.

I would, however, strongly recommend that the number of sub-categories of payment be kept to an absolute minimum and that people who receive such payments, wherever possible, be allowed to manage how they spend their money for themselves. By this I mean, for example that rather than having a separate heating allowance, or radio licence payment etc. there is a universal allowance sufficient to cover all these things and the individual (wherever possible, remember) be responsible for making those payments themselves and be held responsible for any failure to do so. To me that is part and parcel of the educational process and necessary in order that people can understand and contribute properly to a democratic society. Of course there needs to be provision for those who prove incapable, but it should be a last resort and not a knee-jerk reaction or an automatic first default.

Naturally, I understand that such systems could not be implemented overnight, but I believe they are feasible and perhaps sooner rather than later. One objection I can foresee is that local government does not have the systems in place to do all this – especially for people who are not employed or for whom there are no records. While I see that this could be a problem initially, I don't see it as insurmountable, for I think people will very quickly come forward once they see the benefits or be identified if they don't come forward. As for the payment system, I could envisage all payments being handled through an adapted payroll system. I am, therefore, confident it will go a long, long way towards addressing the problems at which we were looking earlier.

WRAP UP

So there you have it: a pretty comprehensive, high-level solution to some of our most pressing societal needs. I am sure that you recognise and understand the need for something, but if you still have to be convinced perhaps the following passage from the Financial Times[42] might finally convince you.

> "Democracy rests on the perception of fair treatment of its citizens. Most people accept the wealth earned by successful business activity. Far less acceptable, however, is the ability of the rich to avoid almost all taxation. The case for a neutral tax system, with few loopholes, is stronger than ever. Regulation must be global. Moreover, such regulation must include taxation. As finance goes global, so must the depth of co-operation among fiscal authorities. A world in which a global plutocratic class pays little or no tax, while benefiting from the stability generated by taxes imposed on the 'little people', will prove unsustainable."

I believe what I am proposing will set us well on the road to a much improved democracy that will accord much more with this. Don't you?

---

[42] Financial Times 25th June 2007

A NEW TAX REGIMEN

CHAPTER THIRTEEN
A NEW DEMOCRACY

> "Democracy is when the people keep the government in check."
>
> **AUNG SAN SUU KYI**

How far from Lincoln's original definition of democracy as government "of the people, by the people and for the people" Suu Kyi's statement seems. Yet it is perhaps not as ideologically removed as it may at first appear.

Government, by definition, includes authority – an executive power over others that is, ultimately, either taken or given. In either case there is an element of willing or unwilling acceptance which may be either active or passive. At the end of the day, however, to retain its power any government has to look after the interests of its people. Thus government inevitably also includes accountability as well as authority, but democracy alone recognises that accountability and attempts to provide the safeguards to ensure it; and, even though government is by the people, that still means the people have to keep it in check.

Clearly, as we have seen, this has not been happening.

If democracy were working properly:

- Government could not have grown as big as it has;
- Debt could not have soared to the astronomical levels it has; and
- The wealth gap could not have grown as wide as it has.

All three of these situations are contrary to the basic tenets of democracy and could not have happened if:

- Government was truly *for* the people; and
- People were able to keep government in check.

The last two chapters have given a possible solution as to how to turn this around.

Firstly, the idea of universal employee ownership will go a considerable way to curtailing the arrogance, extravagance and excesses of executive management and their extraordinary earnings, which, judging by the examples we have seen and the sticky economic situation, in which we find ourselves, are entirely undeserved. It will provide a framework to truly envelope, engender and enhance the collective intelligence within an organisation and ultimately optimise its performance. Furthermore, the labour dividend finally provides an equitable reward system that will ensure this collective is suitably rewarded for its efforts. Now you have commerce of the people, by the people and for the people. This takes democracy out of the political arena which has until now been its exclusive domain and brings it into the workplace, which can only be a good thing.

Secondly, the idea of a single rate tax system with taxes levied only on employees will go a considerable way towards addressing falling government revenues by addressing both the tax avoidance issue and the off-shoring issue. Of course the idea of a single rate tax system is hardly new, but the conventional wisdom of the progressive system is never challenged as fundamentally undemocratic. Rather, the dubious argument that people who earn more are morally obliged to contribute more has become so ingrained that few dare to argue against it for fear of being denounced as amoral, self-serving and exploiting the less fortunate. The idea of no longer taxing corporate profits, however, but instead taxing employees who earn more as a result of organisational success opens up the question for a more thorough examination. This approach not only reinforces democratic principles, but also takes taxes out of the management equation, meaning they are no longer a consideration, so freeing up management to focus all their attention on their primary responsibilities.

That alone offers a number of additional positives which I will discuss more fully later. For now I just want to focus on democratic implications of this solution.

DISTRIBUTED LEADERSHIP

This employee ownership model brings democracy to the workplace in a couple of ways.

Firstly, it uniquely melds personal and self-interest to create shared values and foster a common purpose. At the organisational (micro-economic) level it means that you have everyone working together as part of an inter-locking single team, with the line-of-sight that comes with that. You now have people who understand and are committed to doing what is best for the business, and who do not need the constant "command and control" performance monitoring and micro-managing of the past.

Ricardo Semler wrote, "Control is passé and a badge of incompetence."[43] The implications here for the success of your business are profound, because you are creating an environment in which "workers do not leave their brains at the front door or factory gate." This means that instead of focusing on performance measures Management can focus on building the business strategically or, as Semler once again so adeptly put it, you create "an environment in which others make decisions and you no longer have to make them yourself."[44]

This is because, in a single step, you have created the autonomy and purpose that are recognised as being as being two of the three most powerful intrinsic motivators, as well as built the foundation for them to willingly pursue the third – mastery. This moves responsibility and decision-making down the line – an essential requirement in a rapidly changing world – and cements cohesion, centres communication and compels collaboration, improving productivity and delivering better results. You are creating a shift away from the

---

[43] Maverick: Introduction Page xiii
[44] Ibid Page 3

existing mentality (at least in the UK and possibly in other countries too) that "if you are bright you don't go into business - you go into financial services." Hopefully this can inspire the re-evaluation and re-generation of industry and the restoration of a more diverse economy.

Secondly, and perhaps even more importantly, this democratisation of the workplace removes the dichotomy between the historic autocracy of business and democracy which creates an inevitable barrier to employee engagement. It fosters a greater and almost universal understanding of how things work. It educates people in both democracy and commerce and thus creates a more aware electorate and thus one that is potentially more capable of making rational decisions at the macro-economic level that will deliver better government.

DISTRIBUTED DEMOCRACY

This last point is reinforced by the proposed changes to the tax system. This creates a more direct and, therefore, more visible connection between work, reward and tax, and so goes some way toward addressing the divide between commerce and economics. It brings the two together in a way that is not currently possible and facilitates a fresh look at the way we govern.

Eliminating tax for companies and instead taxing people where they work can simplify the geography of tax collection, as well as the insane complexity increasingly associated with it. Taxing individuals means that tax is collected where the people work or reside, and can be readily – and more importantly, exclusively – done through the pay-as-you-earn (PAYE) system. This offers a number of practical advantages:

- The legislation to ensure proper collection of the full entitlement already exists and needs little or no changes.
- The systems are already in place to administer the collection process.

- It minimises the likelihood of tax avoidance, especially if collection is kept separate from all other administration, as it should be.
- It means taxes can be collected sooner, more simply and more regularly than at present – thus improving government cash flows and minimising the short term borrowing needs, together with the cost of tax collection.
- With the dependence on profit removed, revenues will be less impacted by economic downturns and massive fluctuations from one year to the next will also be less extreme, making administration easier.

Of course this greater efficiency will reduce the amount of money that government needs and help keep rates lower, which in the present climate is no small thing. Perhaps its biggest advantage, however, is that it enables the inversion of the present system of tax.

Now instead of central government taking its share of tax revenues first before making money available locally, this can be reversed and tax receipts distributed "bottom up." In other words, rather than getting what central government feels it can afford, local government can get the first slice of the cake as I first suggested in *A Feeling of Worth*. This will facilitate what I call distributed democracy and reverse the problem of "upside-down democracy" that I identified earlier.

Remember our fourth principle: there is only one tax payer – something that even Margaret Thatcher as Prime Minister recognised and acknowledged. At present taxes are levied through a number of different channels, including:

- National Income Tax;
- Provincial or state income tax, where appropriate;
- VAT;
- Excise and other duties;
- Road taxes;
- Municipal rates;
- Etc.

No matter where or how the tax is levied, however, it is you and I who end up paying it – directly or indirectly. Have you ever tried to calculate exactly how much of your income actually goes to pay taxes?

Well, that's all very well but why should central government, the level that is furthest removed from tax payer, have "first dibs" on what we pay? Not only does this encourage the profligate behaviour and the type of growth in government I have been challenging, but it creates a strain between local and central government that is coming increasingly to the fore in these straitened times.

If you accept the premise that it is society's response to safeguard the welfare of its people, and particularly the vulnerable, then surely this has to begin at the community level. Tax should, therefore, go first to the community and then to the wider society. It is forgetting or forsaking this concept that allows ghettos or underprivileged communities with their sub-classes to develop. This is how you get the decline, degradation and deprivation, which enables such underprivileged areas like Detroit in the US and Toxteth in the UK, to develop.

Conventional wisdom will argue that it is precisely to avoid such situations that you need a strong central government and that it only through the redistribution of taxes that central government can finance the re-development of these cultural sinkholes. On the surface that does seem logical, but the fact is that such scenarios persist, despite this so-called power that central government is supposed to wield, so why then persist with a system that is clearly failing? Don't forget that definition of insanity that describes it as doing the same thing over and over and expecting a different result. It is time to escape the forces that would have us certified, especially if we want to earn the respect (and not the curses) of future generations.

The belief in the power of central Government is another facet of the emperor with no clothes. The reality is that central Government actually has little, if any, power to do anything about helping people have and lead better lives. All any Government can do is to change the way it spends taxpayers' money, or change structures. The latter are generally useless and very expensive; the former just add to existing complexity and costs, but because they can't admit that they are powerless, central Governments (by which I mean politicians) keep on doing things to maintain the pretence that they can make a difference. The reality is that it is only at the local level that things can be done that make a difference, and that needs both freedom from central interference and greater funding.

I was amazed to discover the extreme frustration that exists in NHS hospitals, when treatments for various illnesses are prescribed in detail in central Government. "If the patient has illness X, give treatment Y." All this does is lead to poorer treatment, as it does not match the highly variable needs of the patient; creates excessive costs through the provision of unnecessary treatments; consumes vast sums of money spent in the centre trying to dictate how professionals look after their patients; and the frustration, which means that people end up going through the motions and not really trying.

Now I am not suggesting that central government does not have a responsibility to help regenerate these impoverished districts. All I am saying is that it has to start with the community. Government of the people, by the people for the people demands this, but it also demands that the community has to take some responsibility for itself, which would be a lot easier if communities had first rights to both their own revenues and the management of them. The two go hand in hand. That is what true democratic government is – or should be – about, but we have lost sight of that somewhere along the way.

By reversing this tax system in this manner you at least create the platform for improved democracy. People will see the correlation between how their affairs are being managed and the quality of life in their community, thus becoming more involved and more ready to hold their local government accountable.

This will then grow and spread on up to central government, enabling us to once again be able to keep a tighter rein on what government gets up to, supported by a greater economic understanding due to the fact that we are all "business people." John Simon once said, "Democracy encourages the majority to decide things about which the majority is ignorant." This proposal goes a very long way towards rectifying that.

EFFECTIVE GOVERNMENT

It goes further than that, though. This is also an opportunity to start breaking away from the party political system, in which the people who get elected are those who spend the most on advertising, and to move towards a system where those who govern are better qualified to do so.

There is an obvious inextricable link between democracy and economics. Unfortunately it remains more of an unconscious awareness, buried in our minds by the more obvious link between government and economics. Clinton's "It's about the economy" election campaign worked because it explicitly acknowledged the fact that we judge government performance according to our personal economic circumstances. Yet despite this we do not make the link with democracy. That is why we have had the democratic decline I have been depicting and why the economy is now in such a terrible mess. We zig-zag from one party government to another, tacking left and then tacking right, papering over and building upon policy driven legislation that moves us further and further from the destination we would actually like to reach. Maybe Thomas Jefferson was on to something when he suggested to James Madison that "each generation was sovereign, so that the laws made by one generation should expire after about twenty years."[45] Unfortunately perhaps even these exceptionally wise men over-emphasised the importance of laws and failed to recognise and establish sound principles. Maybe one of the reasons that government is so expensive is that it spends so much time creating laws, and the more laws you make, the more people you have breaking them. It is no wonder our prisons are full to bursting!

With a system like the one I am proposing, however, elections would be based more on capability than party affiliations and we could choose between people who have the right mix of vision, adaptability and competency: on merit rather than whichever candidate the party happens to put forward, which can be influenced by such agenda items as gender and ethnic origins for example. If we are voting for people who are required and expected to look after our interests we need to have:

- A clear understanding of what our interests actually are;
- Confidence that the people we are electing understand them to and are capable of looking after them.

Even if what I am proposing needs clarification and refinement (which it undoubtedly does) and does not guarantee these two points, it at least offers a platform for it that is better than anything we currently have. It is the start of a system that will help us enable our future rather than become, or continue to be the powerless victims of a default future shaped by people with no understanding.

---

[45] Page 54: *Founding Brothers: The Revolutionary Generation: Joseph J Ellis* ©2000 Published by Alfred A Knopf (A Pulitzer Prize-winning book)

A NEW DEMOCRACY

CHAPTER FOURTEEN
A NEW SUSTAINABILITY

> "After all, sustainability means running the global environment – Earth Inc. – like a corporation: with depreciation, amortization and maintenance accounts. In other words keeping the asset whole, rather than undermining your natural capital."
>
> **MAURICE STRONG**

This looks like a rather scary call given what we have seen about the way corporations are being run and the, largely justified, criticisms of the short-term thinking that dominates current corporate behaviour. There is no doubt that both government and business are facing a credibility crisis after the many scandals that have come to light and the apparent lack of ethics and, perhaps even worse, the lack of consequences or accountability for such behaviour.

Unfortunately, all this comes at a time when the environment is a concern. Without getting embroiled in the arguments about climate change and the extent to which it is or isn't the result of human behaviour, there can be little doubt that we need to be more aware, and take better care of our planet and its environment and natural resources. Especially at a time when population growth and rising living standards in the hitherto less developed nations means there is a greater demand on these resources than ever before. This makes it imperative that, more than we have ever done in the past, we:

- Use these resources more wisely; and
- Eliminate all waste.

Of course this is considerably easier said than done. Yet the increasing recognition of the need to "be more green" and take better care of our world and the environment for the sake of all its inhabitants, is a force that impels even greater centralisation of power, which runs counter to all arguments for less government. Furthermore it is all too easy for the developing countries to argue – not without some justification – that it smacks of self-interest on the part of the developed nations. After all, they have an unprecedentedly high standard of living and now just seem to be trying to prevent others from achieving the same standard. Yet, whether right or wrong, this shouldn't come into the debate. If the developed world has been living beyond its means in terms of its impact on the environment, getting the rest of the world to the same standard is not a viable option – at least not at our present state of technological evolution. Thus we are faced with few options. We could:

1. Develop the technology to better control the climate and redress and reverse the climate change problems we face;
2. Accept a universally lower standard of living than that to which most of us in the developed world have become accustomed;
3. Continue the way we are, bringing the developing countries to the same level as ourselves and accept the consequences, no matter what they are or how extreme they might be;
4. Combine any or all of the above.

Now in reality it is unlikely that any one of these options will provide the sole solution. Rather they will all happen to some degree and it is just the proportion of each that will determine the final outcome. The fact is they all depend on some kind of co-operation and consensus, which in turn demands some kind of framework for enabling it to happen. Consequently the idea of adopting an "Earth, Inc." approach is not so way out and may indeed offer the best way to move forward.

From where I stand, however, the issue remains a global issue and thus needs a global solution. Consequently, the more people you involve (if you like, the more democratic you make the process of trying to solve it) the more effective your solution is likely to be.

The ideas I have expounded in this book offer a good basis for moving forward.

SUSTAINABLE BUSINESS

Intrinsic to the continued existence of any organisation is the role it plays in the community. After all, any organisation, irrespective of its form, is initially founded to meet a want or need. Thus its continued existence should be assured as long as the demand remains and it continues to supply it effectively.

Historically that purpose, combined with an adherence to its legal responsibilities and obligations, has been enough for the organisation to focus on its business with no other concerns and little or no interference. In recent decades, however, there has been wider recognition of the fact that organisations have a greater responsibility to the community/communities in which they operate. As a result there has been increased recognition of the "triple bottom-line," and the term "Corporate Social Responsibility or CSR" has entered the phrase-book. As a result most major organisations report on their CSR initiatives in their annual reports.

This has been driven by the almost reckless lack of regard for natural resources, and the ecological problems this has caused, and the consequent concern about the environment. Sustainability has thus become a major global issue, evidenced by the "green" movement and increasingly widespread efforts of organisations to be "greener." However, there is more to sustainability than just impact on the environment and popular initiatives to prove caring credentials, and there is a great danger that this focus on the environment creates too narrow a focus and ignores some of the wider implications of the concept of sustainability.

Any organisation needs to focus on the long-term, both as a provider and a consumer of resources. Thus, while sustainability definitely includes safeguarding the environment and doing more to protect it, it also includes a moral obligation to optimise its own use of resources. This in turn has a significant two-fold implication for it means that, regardless of their nature, form or structure, organisations need to:

- Be more aware of their external dealings and ensure that all their dealings are principled, positive and proactive.
- Monitor their internal operations more closely and ensure that they are as ethical, efficient and effective as they possibly can be, as well as environmentally aware.

Most organisations have recognised this, and are working on both fronts to improve their contribution. The single overarching aspect to both these, however, is the need for long-term thinking and this is something that is still not being fully recognised or addressed. Think back to the example of Barclays and its tax avoidance business, and how detrimental this is to the wider economy and its own long-term prospects. This is typical of the short-termism that is so prevalent and why organisations need to pay more attention to the long-term. It is only possible to ensure that sustainability efforts are not wasted by placing a greater emphasis on the long-term. To create the concerted effort to safe-guard sustainability and ensure this kind of long-term thinking requires everyone to be thinking more about the long-term.

This means that looking after the long-term cannot be the responsibility of the executive team alone, but has to be spread throughout the organisation. My employee ownership model does this in two ways:

1. It compels the organisation to place greater value on its people as a key asset; and
2. Through the distributed leadership it generates through the sense of ownership.

Thus you have not only melded personal and self-interest to create shared values and foster a common purpose but, because all employees are concerned about the future of the organisation and hence its business, you also have a natural interest in and concern about the community it serves.

This has another benefit too because it tempers the authority of the people at the top. It reduces the likelihood of mergers and the reduced value that they create that we discussed earlier. While it may not totally preclude the possibility of massive ethical failures such as Enron and its ilk, it means that you have more people involved and thus a greater likelihood of somebody speaking out. This also reduces the risk of surprises, and the kinds of sudden collapses when major corporations fail. It thus makes the organisation itself more sustainable and potentially reduces the scale and impact of corporate failure, both for employees and the wider stakeholder community.

AN EDUCATED ELECTORATE

Remember Thomas Jefferson's words, "Democracy demands an educated and informed electorate"? Well this solution gives you just that: it provides just what you need for his corollary statement, "When people are well-informed, they can be trusted with their own government." It does this because it gives you people who, because they are all business people, by virtue of being owners in the employer organisations, understand how business works. They will, therefore, inevitably also have a simultaneous understanding of how government works, because at the end of the day government is not all that different from being a business. After all business is, in essence, an organisational activity carried out to provide a product or service to people in the most efficient and effective way possible. Thus they will be better able to understand the broader issues and to vote more sensibly.

I don't know about you, but I know that I have only one vote and I would be a lot more comfortable knowing that my government, even if it isn't the one I voted for, was elected by people who really understood how they were voting and why, rather than following a tradition because they've always voted for the xyz party (and in some cases because their parents also always voted for xyz party!)

There is too much at stake and the risks are too high for us to have anything but the most effective government we can get. If we are to save the planet and enable a better future that leaves a worthwhile legacy to our descendants, then we need a smarter electorate that understands what it is they are doing, and this approach will do more than anything we currently have in place to enable that.

EPILOGUE

"Democracy isn't a gift. It's a responsibility."
DALTON TRUMBO

If you think about it, there is nothing unduly profound in this statement of Trumbo's. It is simply the entirely natural and inevitable consequence of democracy. How on earth are you ever going to get a government "of the people, by the people, and for the people" if people do not accept what it means, remain vigilant and act responsibility?

Hopefully you are already aware that democracy is under constant attack. There are, and always will be, people who think they stand to gain more by looking out only for themselves and their interests and for whom democracy is an inconvenience or worse. Notwithstanding the fact that, paradoxically, it is democracy that more than likely makes their situation possible, they either remain indifferent to it or actively or passively work to undermine it. Either can be deadly for democracy in the long-term, but this danger grows when self-interest spreads and becomes dominant in society, which unfortunately is precisely what has been happening in recent years.

It was Mikhail Gorbachev who said, "Democracy must learn to defend itself," and he could be described as a relatively late arrival at the party. Yet he seemed to have a better understanding of that imperative than many of us, although there is an awful lot said and written about the subject. Someone else, however, who also seemed to both understand this and have a better idea of how to go about it was Alfred E Smith who stated that "All the ills of democracy can be cured by more democracy."

In a way that rather encapsulates the essence of this book. I have tried to point out how democracy has been, and is being, eroded while at the same time proposing more democratic solutions for dealing with the problem. One of the few ways that you can address the effects of erosion is to strengthen and replenish what is being eroded, and that is effectively what I have tried to do.

In doing so I have tried to avoid the trap of being "the perpetual doubter" who is "a nitpicking needle-snout who can always find a problem and happily pick holes in the solutions of others"[46] and rather put forward some constructive suggestions that could provide a new way forward. So I do hope you will give me the credit for that even if you don't agree with the ideas themselves. That hope, however, pails into insignificance beside the greater hope that you will actually believe the ideas have merit and help champion them, so that we can all contribute to a lasting legacy and enable a future that is better, brighter and more brilliant than anything that currently looks feasible.

Reinhold Niebuhr once said that, "Democracy is finding proximate solutions to insoluble problems." It would therefore be foolhardy as well as extremely presumptuous of me to even begin to claim that I have found a panacea that proves him wrong, if for no other reason than defending democracy is a day-to-day demand and a never-ending one at that. But I hope that some of the ideas will make the task that much easier for those who have to continue the battle after us.

---

[46] A delightful expression I encountered in a newsletter from the "Wizard of Ads", Roy H Williams.

AFTERWORD

"No one knows anything about economics. It is the great lie of economists."
VINCENTE DEL BOSQUE

I have no idea of the context of those words but I cannot help thinking that they are more apt than anyone would want to believe.

Some readers of this book, including Lawrence Bloom, have suggested that it does not go far enough in challenging some of the more basic elements of economics, and, in particular, the use of GDP as the primary economic measure. There were two very good reasons for this:

- I freely admit to being one of those people who does not know much about economics and therefore I felt it would be too presumptuous to do so.
- My inability to offer any feasible alternative.

While the book does address many economic issues they are simply my own observations on what I perceive is happening in the world around me, and so I made a conscious an effort not to criticise without putting forward what I believe are constructive solutions for redressing those shortcomings.

Thus I chose to focus instead on the more commercial aspects of economics and, in particular, the significant gap between commerce and economics. The example of laying off people during an economic downturn when it simply transfers the cost from the organisation to the community is a key symptom of this. Consequently I pulled my punch on these other aspects, hoping (as they have) that astute readers would pick up on the issue any way. Instead I consciously focused on the elements where I felt I could be more original, more credibly constructive and (hopefully) add more value.

Nevertheless the point is valid, and I am glad that it has been raised. GDP as a primary economic measure is seriously flawed and our preoccupation with it is dangerous. This is exemplified by the fact that between 2009 and 2015, a time when most of the UK was experiencing a significant decline in their living standards and real incomes, the super-rich *more than doubled* their wealth. This undoubtedly reflected in the national statistics with GDP indicating a growing economy when the population at large was struggling and, from their perspective, definitely facing the opposite.

This dichotomy supports the points I have been making. When the "average" person earning £25,000 per year would have to work for 526,800 years to amass the wealth of the wealthiest person you have to agree that there is an imbalance. Perhaps it was always like this, but it would seem that the deck is being stacked even more in favour of the wealthy. As I have said, if such disparity continues to flourish and grow, it creates a deadly threat to the civil and stable society that (most of us) currently enjoy. To actively promote it goes beyond being irresponsible and becomes insane, and makes revolution virtually inevitable. As I shall highlight shortly, we may be on the fringes of such a revolution even now.

Furthermore, my example of the company that had reduced its headcount by 110,000 people, with the consequential cost savings being more than the growth in its profits, supports this. It also to some extent supports Karl Marx's statement that, "The production of too many useful things results in too many useless people."

While I would not go so far as saying it makes people "useless" (the word is too subjective and pejorative) there are good grounds for arguing that our technological progress is placing additional strain on long term employment prospects. The development of robotics and artificial intelligence may reduce human input and increase unemployment even further, making "full employment" a pipe dream. Certainly it will change the nature of work dramatically. This demands proactive thinking to:

- Develop new, more inclusive systems for distributing work;
- Educate and equip the workforce – especially the younger generation who, statistics show, have been hardest hit by these socio-economic shifts.
- Anticipate and prevent an apocalyptic, Orwellian future.

Even more importantly though, it also demands new economic measures, for it is absolutely insane to keep looking at national productivity when so many people are unemployed or under-employed. Although people are increasingly calling for this, no-one seems to recognise the paradox between the demand for greater productivity and increased employment, which are, fundamentally, mutually exclusive objectives.

I thus hope that *The Democracy Delusion* will strengthen the case for such efforts and therefore play a constructive part in doing so, but I leave others to make that case more effectively than I can and to come up with new, better measures that elude me. Goodness knows we need to!

Yet since first penning the book in the hope of giving a useful insight into the manner in which our basic values have been, and are being, subverted and some possible solutions for redressing the issues, I have learned of new threats. As a result I am now growing concerned that it may already be too late. These are more serious and imminent than anything I was previously aware of. The very fundamentals of democracy are being actively and wilfully destroyed, and there is now a greater need for urgency to safeguard our values as well as to make systemic changes to our social and economic model. This threat is serious and goes beyond eroding democracy and not only threatens our freedoms and that of future generations, but our very existence.

Let me tell you about this new threat.

THE TRANSATLANTIC BUSINESS DIALOGUE (TABD)

Formed in 1995 by the US government and the European Union (EU) the TABD was the official business sector advisory group for EU and US officials on trade and investment issues. The objective was to establish an ongoing discussion between international business and governments at the highest level and "to create an official forum that allowed these transatlantic businesses to come together in a single setting where they would be able to address their mutual concerns."[47]

Given the economic clout that these organisations have you could argue that this was a logical step. On the other hand you could also argue that effectively gives "big business" a place at the government table and as such shows a blatant disregard for democracy.

This might be alright if what is good for business is automatically good for the people but, unfortunately, that is the misguided thinking behind much economic policy, and, as we have seen with the recent banking and other scandals, this link is not something you can take for granted. You cannot perhaps help even wondering if this laid the foundations for the global financial crisis in 2008 by giving the financial services industry a sense of being above the law. Regardless it was only the beginning, for 2007 saw the creation of the Transatlantic Economic Council to press for free trade based on the deregulation of markets in the USA and EU and gave the TABD a platform for its ultimate goal of establishing a barrier-free transatlantic market.

Then in January 2013 the TABD was merged with the European-American Business Council, which had been formed in 1997 as the successor to the European Community Chamber of Commerce in the United States, to form the Transatlantic Business Council (TABC.) This is an advocacy group of more than 70 multinational businesses, which continues to operate with the TABD as a major strategic programme. It would therefore be entirely natural for these organisations to lobby for their own best interests and that seems to be the case for the results of their labours has inevitably led to controversy and criticism, and to such an extent that the subtle

---

[47] https://en.wikipedia.org/wiki/Transatlantic_Business_Dialogue

attack on basic democracy in this collection of entirely democratic countries generates very little attention.

So let us explore why that is.

THE TRANSATLANTIC TRADE & INVESTMENT PARTNERSHIP (TTIP)

Most of this controversy is focussed around the Transatlantic Trade and Investment Partnership (TTIP). This is a proposed trade agreement between the USA and the EU and stems from the work of the TABD.

In April 2012 the US Business Roundtable, the European Round Table of Industrialists and the TABD issued a joint statement, 'Forging a Transatlantic Partnership for the 21st Century'[48] calling for an ambitious trade and investment partnership between the EU and USA. Specifically this stated that this "should not be just another free trade agreement; it should be a more ambitious and relevant new-generation accord, rooted in the distinctive nature and potential of the transatlantic partnership. In addition to being grounded in essential principles of WTO-consistency, transparency, and non-discrimination among the parties, it should advance synergistic strategies across a range of areas, from removing tariff and non-tariff barriers to transatlantic trade in industrial and agricultural goods and services, removing restrictions on job-creating investments, further opening of the public procurement market, *overcoming regulatory obstacles*, [my emphasis] boosting innovation, encouraging the flow of people and talent across the transatlantic space to addressing emerging 21st Century issues like facilitating cross-border data flows which have become essential to global manufacturing and services operations."

Firm believers of Arnold Gasgow's words, "An idea not coupled with action will not get any bigger than the brain

---

[48] http://ec.europa.eu/enterprise/policies/international/cooperating-governments/usa/jobs-growth/files/consultation/regulation/10b-br-tabd-ert-annex_en.pdf

cell it occupied," as well as their own demand to achieve "each of the core objectives outlined in this paper to the maximum extent and as quickly as possible," a group of high-level experts submitted their findings on 11 February 2013[49] and recommended launching negotiations for a wide free-trade agreement.

With almost supernatural efficiency President Barack Obama called for such an agreement in his state of the Union address the next day (12 February 2013), while the following day EU Commission president José Manual Barroso announced that talks would take place to negotiate an agreement.[50] TTIP had been born.

This speed was mirrored in the negotiations where negotiators worked to a deadline of reaching agreement by the end of 2015. And it is not just businesses that were in such a hurry. President Obama claimed that his administration was "reinvigorating efforts" while UK Prime Minister David Cameron called for "rocket boosters" and German Chancellor Angela Merkel proclaimed, there was "no time to lose."[51] (As an aside, one has to question the grasp of the situation when you consider that at the same time as promoting this deal, David Cameron was also fighting an election with a campaign manifesto of a referendum on whether the UK should remain a part of the EU or not. If he does understand, then he is being shamefully dishonest.) Understandably this haste to reach agreement has been a major battle line for opponents of the proposal. Especially when you consider some of the other issues.[52]

---

[49] https://en.wikipedia.org/wiki/Transatlantic_Trade_and_Investment_Partnership
[50] Ibid
[51] Financial Times report by World Trade Editor Shawn Donnan, 16 December 2014 http://www.ft.com/cms/s/0/b8352156-843f-11e4-bae9-00144feabdc0.html#axzz3eXA2J34a
[52] The headings I have used are taken straight from: The Transatlantic Trade and Investment Partnership: A charter for deregulation, an attack on jobs, an end to democracy. 2015 update: by John Hilary. This is possibly the most succinct and comprehensive explanation of TTIP and its issues.

Transparency and democracy denied

Not surprisingly, the first rallying point of opponents is the lack of transparency and democracy in the negotiations. What is perhaps surprising is how little focus is given to the fact that the parties to the negotiations have no democratic rights to represent the citizens of the countries involved and therefore no accountability to any electorate. This is a long way removed from the principles of government *by* the people *for* the people.

Opponents are making an issue of the lack of transparency involved in the negotiations and the lack of democracy that this entails. But inevitably proponents of the agreement claim this is a myth and point to the opposition and criticism that the talks have generated to support their case. Yet, to any impartial observer trying to form an objective opinion on the subject, this lack of transparency does seems real.

Even the EU Ombudsman has called for greater transparency around the lobbying involved in TTIP while the Independent UN expert on the promotion of a democratic and equitable international order, Alfred de Zayas, is reported to have said, "I am concerned about the secrecy surrounding negotiations for trade treaties, which have excluded key stakeholder groups from the process, including labour unions, environmental protection groups, food-safety movements and health professionals. Proactive disclosure by governments, genuine consultation and public participation in decision-making are indispensable to make these agreements democratically legitimate. 'Fast-tracking' adoption of such treaties has a detrimental impact on the promotion of a democratic and equitable world order."[53]

If proponents of the deal truly believe it is in everyone's best interests and not just their own, then they should have no issue with more openness and frank discussion.

---

[53] EU ombudsman pans TTIP talks over lack of transparency
http://sputniknews.com/europe/20150511/1021989239.html

Negative economic and employment impacts

Proponents of TTIP claim that it will bring major benefits to all, while their opponents claim the opposite. Which naturally begs the question, "Who is right?"

The following table, reproduced from an April 2015 New Economic Forum (NEF) blog entitled "Does TTIP really make economic sense?"[54] presents the findings of 5 different research studies on the long term effects of TTIP on the EU (by 2027) and shows that there is a large discrepancy in the assessment of the potential benefits.

INDICATOR	CEPR (2013)	CEPII (2013)	Ecorys (2009)	Bertelsmann (2013)	Capaldo (2014)
Exports (% change)	5.9%	7.6%	0.9%	No estimate	Estimates for selected countries
GDP (% change)	0.49%	0.30%	0.34%	No estimate	Estimates for selected countries
Employment (# of jobs)	Assumes fixed amount of labour; 1,300,000 due to displacement of labour	Not discussed	Assumes fixed amount of labour	1,300,000	-583,000

Given these findings, which seem to include both the most optimistic and the most pessimistic, it is hard to disagree with the conclusion drawn: "All of these are long-term impacts so we know very little about what effects will be experienced before 2027, in particular for jobs and wages. Yet even the long-term outcomes are hardly what one would imagine a 'comeback for Europe' to look like. The same is true when we look at modelled impacts for individual countries."[55]

If you factor in the inadequacy of GDP as an economic measure for the whole of society and the likelihood that the recent growth in UK GDP, at a time when the majority were experiencing a decline in their living standards, was entirely due to the wealthier getting even wealthier, you have to wonder if this growth will not once again be due to the same phenomenon. In other words, will it be the wealthy who benefit most from the proposed agreement?

---

[54] http://www.neweconomics.org/blog/entry/does-ttip-really-make-economic-sense
[55] Ibid

Certainly, given some of the other concerns, it would be foolhardy to rush into any agreement without a proper in depth analysis of the benefits. Especially if you take into account the fact that, rather like weather forecasters, economists have a poor track record of predicting the future.

Deregulation at the heart of TTIP

This is an area where opponents to TTIP definitely have the high ground. As you saw "overcoming regulatory barriers" is enshrined in the original proposal by TABD and is part of what makes TTIP such an ambitious concept and moves it beyond being a 'routine' free trade agreement.

Many of these so-called 'barriers' represent the most important measures to protect the environment and public health and safety. Indeed Europe has been at the forefront of efforts to reduce the impact of climate change and safeguard the environment while the USA has been notoriously recalcitrant in even ratifying global environmental agreements, let alone taking vital steps to protect our planet. Consequently opponents to TTIP are totally justified in sounding the alarm on this issue.

According to them, TTIP "still seeks to 'harmonise' regulatory regimes on both sides of the Atlantic so as to remove unwanted restrictions on business operations, with the effect of undermining higher social and environmental standards in Europe so as to ensure regulatory 'coherence', 'convergence' or 'alignment' with the USA. In the face of opposition to such an agenda the European Commission has focused on the possibility of introducing 'mutual recognition of standards' via TTIP, thereby granting equivalence to the USA's regulatory regime even when it is less exacting than its European counterpart. This would place European companies at an immediate disadvantage with US competitors and would lead to an inevitable race to the bottom in regulatory standards."[56]

---

[56] Source: The Transatlantic Trade and Investment Partnership: A charter for deregulation, an attack on jobs, an end to democracy. 2015 update: John Hilary, citing 'TTIP

Even if you are a climate change sceptic and regard it as a hoax, common sense or basic humanity should make you pause to consider what happens if you are wrong. Taking steps to protect the planet and safeguard it for our fellow inhabitants (on whom our own existence ultimately depends) and future generations makes total sense. Furthermore, it also opens up the prospect of a whole new swathe of opportunities and potential 'green' jobs and income streams. On the other hand disregarding any warnings is to risk jeopardising any kind of future for anyone and anything and leaving our planet as yet another lifeless form travelling through space.

The nature of business is such that you can ultimately only increase returns in one of three ways – increasing sales, cutting costs or introducing more effective processes. Businesses operating on a global basis under the same set of rules will thus inevitably do everything in their power to achieve any or all of these three things. This makes the "race to the bottom" in terms of sustainability and safeguarding environment resources a very real proposition. For me that is a risk too far.

Public services under threat

One of the other major concerns with TTIP is the extent to which it opens up all aspects of the economy to competition. "The EU's initial liberalisation 'offer' to the USA, leaked in June 2014, confirms that medical and health services, social services, education (at all levels), post, finance, communications, transport, energy, water, environmental and cultural services are all on the table in TTIP, with substantial commitments already in place across many sectors to allow US corporations full access to the services markets of EU member states."[57]

Whether this is a threat depends on your perspective, but there is no doubt that this effectively means opening up public sector services to competition and thus raises the spectre

---

1. Draft services/investment offer. 2. US State level measures' Brussels: European Commission 26 May 2014 Page 11
[57] Ibid Page 13

of 'privatisation' by any other name. In any event, the idea of doing this without any approval to do so by the electorate is undemocratic in the extreme.

ISDS – in both TTIP and CETA

The provision for Investor-State Dispute Settlement (ISDS) in TTIP and its Canadian counterpart, the Canada-Europe Trade Agreement (CETA), is unquestionably the biggest threat to democracy of all – and perhaps the biggest threat since the Magna Carta over 800 years ago.

This threat is perhaps best explained in a report in the EU parliamentary magazine, *The Parliament*, by Julie Levy-Abegnoli dated 7 May 2015.[58] As the headline, "No TTIP deal with ISDS, warns parliament" suggests, members of the European Parliament (MEPs) are saying that despite revised plans, they will block TTIP if ISDS is included.

Initial opposition arose because "with an ISDS system in place, corporations would be able to challenge governments in a private trade tribunal. There are concerns that such a system would give companies excessive power over national authorities and allow them to sue governments every time legislation was introduced that might harm their profits."

The report states, "Attempting to put these fears to rest, European Trade Commissioner Celia Malmström had negotiated a revised ISDS plans, which, she told MEPs, were intended 'to remove any ambiguity about sovereign governments' right to regulate, putting that in black and white.' She explained that, 'In the past, agreements have been drafted more with the protection of investment in mind than the right of governments to regulate – this will no longer be the case.' The commission's ultimate goal, was to establish 'a permanent international investment court,' she said, admitting that this would take some time to establish."

It continues, "In the new ISDS system, arbitrators would be selected from a pre-vetted list agreed upon by the EU and

---

[58] https://www.theparliamentmagazine.eu/articles/news/no-ttip-deal-isds-warns-parliament

US, and with both sides '*setting the qualification requirements to become an arbitrator at the same level as those of judges.*' [My emphasis again; stressing how this puts the arbitrators outside and above the national legal system.] Malmström has also proposed to implement 'a multilateral appeal mechanism as part of a permanent court.'"

"Insisting that these were 'not cosmetic changes but rather the most significant overhaul of investment arbitration in decades', the commissioner rejected calls to take investment arbitration out of TTIP, saying, 'this just doesn't make sense'."

"She pointed out that 'US courts are not obliged to follow commitments that the US takes internationally. And the US does not always respect its international commitments', arguing that, 'Canada, and soon Japan and China, has the safety net of effective investment arbitration with the US, why shouldn't Europeans have that?'"

It seems to me that the MEPs are quite right to take a stance against ISDS in its entirety. What you have here is the arbitrary creation of a new legal system outside of the traditional court systems of the countries involved, and created without any direct reference to the electorates of the countries involved.

The first line of defence against this is the MEPs and one has to have misgivings as to how long they will stand up to any intensive lobbying by the business organisations promoting the agreement.

The second line of defence is the requirement for all member states to ratify this before it can take effect. This is something that I would not like to put to the test, especially if this is not presented as a major change to the European Charter. The risk of it coming into effect by the backdoor is not one I would be willing to take, especially after reading about some of the notable examples of ISDS-type principles being built into bilateral trade agreements. Two include:[59]

---

[59] Source: The Transatlantic Trade and Investment Partnership: A charter for deregulation, an attack on jobs, an end to democracy. 2015 update: John Hilary Page 45

- The Swedish energy company Vattenfall suing the German government for €3.7 billion (yes, billion) over the country's decision to phase out nuclear power in the wake of the Fukushuma nuclear disaster! This follows a previous success in challenging the City of Hamburg's environmental regulations, which were watered down in the face of the company's attack. (Remember the 'race to the bottom described earlier? Here is evidence of the risk faced.)
- In another such example, under NAFTA rules Canada was forced to revoke its ban on the fuel additive MMT under a challenge from US company Ethyl. In a later case over water and timber rights, Canada had to pay out $122 million to the Canadian Paper company Abitibi, which sued through its US subsidiary using NAFTA rules.

This is a good introduction into CETA, which is being negotiated concurrently with TTIP and which, because it is not raising the same amount of concern may be ratified before TTIP and why it also presents a threat along the same lines as TTIP. Even if ISDS is removed from TTIP its inclusion in the parallel EU-Canada deal (CETA) means that EU states could already find themselves exposed to multi-billion dollar suits from US corporations. If CETA is ratified "over 80% of US-owned companies will be able to make use of the ISDA provisions included within it by virtue of their subsidiaries in Canada."[60]

Now you can perhaps understand why I made the claim that this could be the biggest danger to democracy since the Magna Carta. That document "established for the first time the principle that everybody, including the king, was subject to the law. Most famously, the 39th clause gave all 'free men' the right to justice and a fair trial. Some of Magna Carta's core principles are echoed in the United States Bill of Rights (1791) and in many other constitutional documents around

---

[60] Ibid Page 16

the world, as well as in the Universal Declaration of Human Rights (1948) and the European Convention on Human Rights (1950)."[61]

TTIP and other similar bilateral agreements nullify this completely. In the name of protecting the investor, they tilt the pendulum too far towards protecting corporate interests and supercede individual and consumer rights. As evidenced by the examples cited they effectively place corporations above the law and give them the right to challenge, amend or bypass any law of a country outside of their own domicile. This, I am sure you will agree, is entirely undemocratic and a risk too far and thus a step that we should not allow to be taken.

There can be little doubt that TTIP corroborates the case I made in Chapter 8 that big business is sabotaging the state, but government complicity is a massive concern. One has to question whether it is due to ignorance or more sinister circumstances.

Yes, generally governments do well when business does well. This simply reflects the "It's all about the economy" logic that underpinned Bill Clinton's presidential campaign. As Henry Ford showed, good business powers a good economy and a higher standard of living for all. Unfortunately recent history shows business is not always good and thus we now need stronger restraints on business; the exact opposite of what TTIP is fostering.

In its aggressive tax avoidance approaches, business has itself broken the bond that business doing well also meant government did well. Now there should no longer be such strong efforts on the part of government to safeguard business interests. Unfortunately conventional wisdom does not seem to have caught up with that reality yet and there is a very real danger that, when the truth does dawn, it will be too late.

That's the ignorance aspect. The more sinister possibility is the power of the lobbyists and whether our politicians are acting in their own best interests rather than ours. Either way

---

[61] Source: The British Library http://www.bl.uk/magna-carta/articles/magna-carta-an-introduction

we have to ensure that this proposed agreement never gets ratified. That is easier done by fighting them with new ideas, rather than personal or political confrontation.

TAKING UP THE CUDGELS

Clearly TTIP ups the ante in our need to safeguard democracy, protect our personal rights, which we have perhaps come to take for granted, and even to safeguard our planet and ensure that we leave future generations a chance to live and lead a life worth living. It is definitely time to take up the cudgels and start fighting.

Our fight, however, will be far more effective if we avoid the very real danger of conducting it along purely ideological grounds.

The people most strongly opposed to TTIP are the trade unionists and people who could be said to be more 'left wing' in their philosophy. To some extent this is only natural, because they are continuing an historical struggle against inhumane 'capitalism' and business as its manifestation. It is a problem, however, because it centres the fight along the old, traditional 'socialist vs capitalist' fault lines, even though, in this instance, there is considerable justification.

If you boil down the whole justification for TTIP, it stems from businesses being frustrated by the more socialistic nature of business as it is conducted in Europe compared to the US. As a result there is a conviction that it is expensive, inefficient and a drag on profits and therefore there is a perceived need to overcome such 'constraints.'

This in itself is largely the result of a misconception of capitalism and a persistent, misplaced faith in the 'self-regulating effect' of markets as the 'invisible hand' as first depicted by Adam Smith. The fallacy of such one dimensional thinking is highlighted by Harvard Business School Professor Bruce R Scott in his 'monograph' "The Concept of Capitalism." In this short book, he states, "Capitalism is a three-level system of indirect governance for economic relationships; it is a system that is political and administrative as well as economic. Organised markets cannot exist without a set of institutional foundations that establish various rights and responsibilities that are attributed to notions of property, and these foundations are created, legitimated, regulated, and periodically modernised under the auspices of a political authority."[62]

He goes on to describe "a 'toxic trio' of policies (i.e. reliance on self-regulation, the adoption of shareholder capitalism as a concept of corporate purpose, and the use of one-way, upside-only incentive compensation) that set the stage for the disaster that was allowed to incubate in an otherwise benign set of circumstances including high employment, steady growth and low inflation."[63]

It is therefore a supreme irony that, just when he is outlining a new "three-level" capitalism, business interests clinging on to the discredited format are not only ignoring the better system that is already operating in Europe to protect and safeguard rights and enforce regulation, but actively seeking to undermine it. We have already seen what damage this approach can create. We cannot allow it to happen again!

Yet the threat is very real. We may be being deluded that the 2008 crisis was an unfortunate blip and won't happen again and that the global economy is back on track, but the Greek crisis is a clear sign that it is not. Greece happens to be in the unfortunate position of being the first country to face bankruptcy as a result of excessive national debt. It is very unlikely to be the last. But events there point to the danger of revolution that I am warning against.

On the surface it may look as though the Greek people are playing King Canute, and trying to hold back the tide of 'austerity' – the natural consequence any debtor faces when attempting to get their finances back on track. No matter who you are such efforts inevitably entail a decline in living standards. The Greeks, are now facing a situation where the gap between what they have become accustomed to and

---

[62] The Concept of Capitalism: Chapter 7.
[63] Ibid: Chapter 8

what they are now expected to adapt to, is no longer reasonable or realistic.

Of course they have to shoulder the responsibility of their seemingly thoughtless borrowing. Greek debt grew like Topsy to the point where it reached 135% of GDP. This is equivalent to you or me borrowing 135% of our annual income and begs the question of what sort of lender would allow this? Can you imagine your bank lending you that kind of money? The net result of this is that it left the Greeks facing a very real "Merchant of Venice" scenario. They were in the ludicrous situation of needing to borrow more money to pay back earlier loans. At this point the terms appeared to be excessive and their lenders decided to say, "No more!" As a result the Greeks then found themselves facing Shylock demanding his money back or his pound of flesh.

With no chance of repaying the money they had no option but to pay the pound of flesh. This means that Greece has effectively lost control of her national affairs. Greece has become the first country in the world to be run by non-governmental financial bodies. Overnight the Greek people have moved from being citizens to serfs in their own country. So where does democracy fit into that scenario?

Yes the Greek government and the Greek people have to shoulder some of the culpability for letting things get to this stage, but so too do their creditors. Traditionally lenders bear the risk of lending. And equally traditionally lenders have always attempted to mitigate their losses. It would seem, however, that such measures have reached historically unprecedented levels and now there is no risk to lending, no matter how foolish the risk.

The danger is that Greece could be just the first. Excessive national debt, as I wrote earlier, is now a global problem. The world, nearly every single nation, has an excessive debt burden, and there is therefore a real chance that Greece could simply be the first country to find itself in this situation. As I wrote earlier, it is very difficult for someone like me to identify just who Shylock is, but it has to be the powers behind the lenders. And there is a danger that, if ISDS comes into being, some large corporation could tip over the economy of any other country that does not 'toe its line' and so create a similar situation. This is the very real risk of unregulated commercial powers being granted to the financial services companies who have been allowed to create money virtually at will. It is therefore time to put an end to all this and to limit the power we give to corporations. It is our turn to say, "No more!"

Consequently we need to join the ranks and actively oppose both TTIP and CETA. We should, however, do so on the grounds that it is fundamentally undemocratic rather than on any ideological basis.

FIGHTING SMARTER

While I am extremely grateful for the good work that opponents of TTIP and CETA have done in raising the alarm and identifying the different dangers that these agreements present, I am a little concerned that they may be being enveloped in the old ideological issues and thus may not be as effective as they could be.

These concerns are flagged by two inextricably linked things:

- The recurrence of the terms 'privatisation' and 'austerity' in their arguments; and
- Comments I regularly hear about anti-capitalist protestors as 'whackos' who are against progress.

The first seems to be continuation of the arguments that lost the 2015 UK general election. Bill Clinton was right when he said, "It's all about the economy." It does not matter what their ideological persuasions are, people will ultimately vote for whoever they think will better protect their livelihoods. Reasonable people are not too concerned about how their public services are delivered as long as their needs are met. Similarly, they also understand all too well that, like people, no nation can continue to live beyond its means indefinitely. Consequently while they do not welcome or enjoy the belt-tightening or deprivation that goes with economic realignment, they understand that it is a necessary and unavoidable evil. (Witness the 2015 UK election result.) In such an environment 'austerity' may be a beacon only to those who really don't understand.

This is exacerbated by resorting to protest as the means to make the case. Whether protestors feel so powerless that they have come to consider protest as the only way that they can make their case is a moot point. Unfortunately it has perhaps been overused as a tactic to the extent that others increasingly ignore them. This may be why anti-capitalist protestors are often seen as 'whackos' and the message gets lost behind the means of delivery.

Whether I am right or wrong about this doesn't really matter; I am just reporting and interpreting subjective feedback I have encountered. The point is that, tying opposition to TTIP with capitalism and/or anti-austerity measures, without offering any alternative suggestions, unreasonably narrows the scope of the battle. Those who are pre-disposed towards capitalism will shrug off the arguments and you will continue preaching to the choir. To gain a new audience you have to come up with new arguments. And hopefully this book enables this. Together we can say, "We will not be serfs or slaves!"

GOING GREENER

As already described, one of the major concerns with the proclaimed focus of TTIP being to remove regulatory barriers has to be the potential damage it can do to the environment. I have touched on this already, but it warrants special emphasis.

The "race to the bottom" depicted presents a specific hazard to efforts to prevent climate change catastrophe. The case of the legal suit against the German government is a prime example of why you need to be worried.

Global efforts to reach agreement on measures to reduce the human impact on climate change have been stonewalled and stymied by the failure of the US to ratify any of the hard-fought agreements. You only have to read *The Climate War*[64] to get a glimmer of understanding of why this is. It reveals the extent to which efforts to introduce measures to protect the environment have been continuously and strenuously fought against by opponents who have put commercial interests first. If nothing else, that book exposes the extent to which large corporations lobby, influence and manipulate policy in far more detail than I have described, and, in doing so portrays a much more comprehensive picture of the negative forces undermining democracy than those I have revealed.

It doesn't matter whether you are convinced by the environmentalists' concerns or not. The nature of the issues they raise are so serious that, even if they are unduly pessimistic, as a human being there is no way you should disregard them, let alone oppose them. Yet it seems that there are any number of people who are prepared to sacrifice their future and that of our planet for the benefit of the corporations that employ them and their own financial benefit.

Heaven forbid that these forces entrench their power through TTIP. Yet that is the very real danger that removing regulatory controls and putting investor and corporate interests first could wreak. Europe has been leading the way on the environmental front and their legislative efforts would be seriously undermined and even totally negated if TTIP is allowed to go ahead.

If you rule out corporate greed as a major force the other forces that drive this opposition are:

- Fear of the short-term consequences such as the loss of jobs and rising costs;
- The threat of China overtaking the USA as the major global super-power;
- The previously described ideological clash, underpinned by the (old) capitalist theory that capitalism is best when it is unchecked by regulation

---

[64] "The Climate Wars: True Believers, Power Brokers and the Fight to Save the Earth" by Eric Pooley ©2010 Hachette Books

and that the "invisible hand" of market forces will ensure the best ultimate outcome.

The first of these may be real, but would likely be offset in time by new 'green' opportunities. Even if these take time to evolve and come into being, the nature of the crisis is such that mitigating efforts to compensate in the short-term could be developed, even if this means massive retraining programmes.

The second is possibly inevitable given the natural and human resources available to China, but would be more likely to be prevented if the US re-energised itself and used its innovative capabilities to remedy a model that is widely admitted by many leading thinkers to be broken and unworkable.

And the third brings us back to the point that I was making before; namely that we do ourselves no favours if we continue the historical conflict of ideologies. We are no longer dealing with socialist vs capitalist or 'left' wing vs 'right' wing issues. In fact even identifying the struggle as one to safeguard democracy may be to understate the case. It is about so much more.

THE REAL BATTLE

Ultimately it boils down to a battle for human and civil rights rather than democratic rights. The so-called 'liberalisation' of the markets is a death sentence for true liberalism and the belief in individual rights that underpin civil society as we know it today.

In Chapter 6 I described the perpetual struggle we face to balance individual needs with collective needs – the 'me' versus 'we' conundrum and the apparent societal pendulum that swings between the two extremes. I neglected, however, to mention how fortunate we are to even be in such a position. The fact that we are is evidence of the extent to which individual rights and freedoms underpin our 21st Century value systems: so much so that we never even stop to evaluate them.

In all likelihood we owe this largely to those words in the US Declaration of Independence that underpin the US constitution and which, intentionally or not, have shaped western social, economic and political thinking in the 250 or so years since: "We hold these truths to be self-evident, that all men are created equal, that they are endowed by their Creator with certain unalienable Rights, that among these are Life, Liberty and the pursuit of Happiness."[65]

Yet these "unalienable rights" are now in danger of being made redundant. How can you pursue happiness in an environment where corporations can damage and destroy the environment with impunity, or where non-living wage levels are justified on the grounds of increased competitiveness and greater profits? In my book *A Feeling of Worth*, I argued that we are increasingly losing our sense of self-worth on a treadmill that combines greater personal achievement and acquisition with an abdication of social responsibility. Just imagine how much worse it would be if TTIP came into force and more nations followed the Greek path to serfdom and slavery, simply because we are grateful to have a job.

The paradox is that human beings are more effective, more fulfilled, and achieve more, when they contribute more to their community: when they focus as much on the 'we' as the 'me.' A new corporately controlled society, with its 'people are costs' tradition and focus on perpetually reducing costs, inevitably means that people will be no more than a 'resource' and individual rights will diminish as a result. With the 2012 Gallup Worldwide Employee Engagement Survey[66] indicating that only 13% of employees are actively engaged and that 24% are actively disengaged it seems likely that these opportunity costs will grow – hardly good for sustainability!

It is incredibly ironic that this threat is driven predominantly by the US, despite the fact that it runs counter to their constitution, and is therefore unconstitutional. And therein lies our potentially greatest weapon. This is because the same Declaration of Rights continues from the above, "That when-

---

[65] Source: Transcript of the US government archives:
http://www.archives.gov/exhibits/charters/declaration_transcript.html
[66] http://www.gallup.com/poll/165269/worldwide-employees-engaged-work.aspx

ever any Form of Government becomes destructive of these ends, it is the Right of the People to alter or to abolish it, and to institute new Government, laying its foundation on such principles and organizing its powers in such form, as to them shall seem most likely to effect their Safety and Happiness."[67]

This is the battle that we must now take up to safeguard the future.

ENABLING THE FUTURE

Remember Antione de St. Exupery's edict; "As for the future, your task is not to foresee but to enable it." It is particularly relevant for our generation because we are in the unique position where, if we don't make the right decisions, there will not be *any* future. We will not only destroy ourselves, but possibly our beautiful planet as well, along with so much on it that makes it a miracle.

To do this we have to move beyond the old, unproductive ideological conflicts that have cost untold millions of lives and wasted – and continue to waste – so much of our planet's resources. Breaking this cycle demands a different way of looking at things. This is only possible if we start with principles.

Going back to principles creates the possibility of finding more common ground and so reduces the potential for this ideological conflict. Coming up with new solutions then becomes easier as, hopefully, I have demonstrated in this book. The solutions I proffer:

- Transcend the traditional ideological impasse;
- Balance individual and collective responsibility and so redefine and restore human rights to their rightful place;
- Form the basis of a new system for a better world.

They enable a future. Let's go forward and make it happen.

---

[67] Source: Transcript of the US government archives:
http://www.archives.gov/exhibits/charters/declaration_transcript.html

To that end I leave you with the inspiring words of Glenn Thomas, an employee of Sterling Insights Inc. who wrote them after hearing a talk by his CEO Ray Anderson – someone who did understand what is at stake and the need for sustainability.[68]

Tomorrow's Child

Without a name, an unseen face,
and knowing not your time or place,
Tomorrow's child, though yet unborn,
I met you first last Tuesday morn.

A wise friend introduced us two.
And through his sobering point of view
I saw a day that you would see,
a day for you but not for me.

Knowing you has changed my thinking.
For I never had an inkling
that perhaps the things I do
might someday, somehow threaten you.

Tomorrow's child, my daughter, son,
I'm afraid I've just begun
to think of you and of your good,
though always having known I should.

Begin, I will, to weigh the cost
of what I squander, what is lost,
if ever I forget that you
will someday come and live here too.

---

[68] See Ray Anderson's TED Talk on "The Business Logic of Sustainability" from February 2009:
http://www.ted.com/talks/ray_anderson_on_the_business_logic_of_sustainability?language=en

APPENDIX: PEOPLE AS ASSETS – AN OBJECTION OVERCOME

It is ironic but one of the most common objections I encounter when presenting these ideas is that you cannot treat employees as assets. Perhaps you are in that camp and feeling the same misgivings, so let me see what I can do to overcome your objections.

The first argument against the idea is "People cannot be assets, because you cannot own them!"

This one always takes me aback because, frankly, I see the whole question of ownership as totally irrelevant. The key aspect of the definition of an asset is that the article must have value or perceived value. Now value is always subjective, and a key element of the concept of valuing people is that the method of valuing people must be consistent, and the method I propose for that meets that criterion. It takes the subjectivity out of the equation and leaves little room for conflict once the basics have been understood and agreed, but while ownership is almost invariably included in any definition, it is not something that has to be and so I see it is as a secondary requirement, which can be easily dispensed with.

This is not unprecedented. After all you talk about "your home" and regard it as an asset even if:

- You are only renting; or
- You have just moved in and have a mortgage that technically makes the bank the owner.

Furthermore, businesses are obliged under accounting convention to disclose as assets property that they only lease. So why should it not be possible to apply similar flexibility to an organisation's human assets. The frequency with which people are referred to as assets means the concept at least is pretty widely recognised. Fundamentally all we are talking about here is bringing accounting treatment into line and reducing the risk of executives being seen as hypocritical.

There is, however, an even stronger case that such accounting treatment is not unprecedented. Sportspeople are regarded as, and treated as, assets by the clubs that own them. Musicians and singers are treated as assets by the studio or label to which they are contracted. Actors and actresses are (or used to be) treated as assets by the studios for which they work/worked.

The only difference here is that now, instead of selecting and isolating specific people, you are applying the principles universally. That cannot be a bad thing if you recognise that the organisation can only succeed if everyone plays their full part and it is hardly a stretch of the imagination to view the organisation as a single team. After all if the groundsman doesn't do his job properly a bad bounce could cost his team the league and the few million that ride on it.

The second common objection I encounter is "It is all very well, but you have no control over their movement. People can leave at any time."

This is a practical concern and does, at least theoretically, create something of a challenge. It is, however, only that – a practical concern – and not an insurmountable barrier. Even if it does present a challenge or make life a little more difficult that is no reason to eliminate it as a potential solution. Like many barriers it can be easily dissolved.

In fact the argument that a person could leave at any time is similarly hollow. Any asset can be lost or destroyed at any time. Can you imagine the early merchants who fathered trade as we currently know it, refusing to value their ships or the goods on them, because they could be lost in a storm at any time? The risk of having an employee resign is hardly all that different and of course that risk is considerably reduced if you offer employee ownership as part of their employment contract. Neither do I think an argument that you cannot have people owning themselves adds anything to the earlier debate.

If you think about it, these objections are no more than another example of conventional wisdom. So don't let yourself be conned by either this or a lack of imagination. Organisations treating their people as the assets they really are, offers the key to a whole new economic order, as well as a new impetus to democracy as it should be.

ABOUT THE AUTHOR

Bay Jordan was born and raised in Rhodesia (now Zimbabwe) in the aftermath of Rhodesia's ill-feted Unilateral Declaration of Independence (UDI). Obliged to combine his accountancy studies with mandatory military service in the war that followed, the futility of fighting an ideology with a rifle appalled him. He moved to South Africa as soon as he had finished his final exams but, slightly over a decade later, emigrated with his family to Canada, before transferring to the UK in the mid-nineties. This itinerant history has fuelled Bay's awareness of socio-political issues, but done nothing to convince him about the manner in which they are being tackled. This book is his personal diagnosis of the fundamental flaws with constructive suggestions as to how they can be effectively resolved.

If you'd like to find out more or share your own ideas connect with Bay at www.twitter.com/bayzeal or visit his websites at www.bayjordan.com and www.zealise.com

BY THE SAME AUTHOR

> "The world is a dangerous place; not because of the people who are evil, but because of the people who don't do anything about it."
>
> ALBERT EINSTEIN

A FEELING OF WORTH

A Manifesto For Mending Our Broken World

BAY JORDAN

WWW.BOOKSHAKER.COM

www.ingramcontent.com/pod-product-compliance
Lightning Source LLC
Chambersburg PA
CBHW031952080426
42735CB00007B/363